Bluesy Ballymoe: Pulse and Hearts above Zero

Copyright © William Tiernan, 2018

Dedication

I dedicate this, my second book, once again to my late parents, John Joe and Celia; my late brother, Michael; little Michael, James, little Shane and Big Lall too, and to all our loved ones throughout the whole parish and all the parishes throughout the length and breadth of the country. Their presence was so warm among us and maybe not their passing away so cold.

There are times I wonder what it is all about. I'm a poet, loner in my body and in my soul but in my heart, I'm a people's person.

Also to my brothers, Sean, P.J. and Jimmy; my sisters, Catherine and Eileen.

Acknowledgements

Many thanks to artist, Anne Rigney; to Teresa, Richie Farrell, John Martin Griffin, Martin McHugh, Michael Fitzmaurice, Mary Delaney, Ethna Jarrett, Mary Gordon, Martina and Laura Swift, Mary Mullins. The wonderful caterers who worked their butts off on the night of my last launch: Mary, Imelda, Bernie, Rosaleen, Tina and Marie.

This publication has been made possible thanks to generous sponsorship received from the Arts Office at Roscommon County Council

God bless all of you.

Preface

My Heart is in Guilka – this is a poem I've penned on this second book. Not anymore is it. I am not the victim of tyranny, empty bedroom or an empty house, or idleness, or grief, or casual ignorance, or passing loneliness, or unhappiness. There are, however, dying voices inside me, reaching out almost everywhere and sometimes heard from nowhere; and where, I ask, is nowhere? My brain is in my head but, my mind is just about everywhere. The whole thing about living in Guilka will come to an end in the next three to five years. There is too much sadness about the place. A dying or dead emptiness. It scribbles itself into the places I used to play and those places ache now. Did you ever hurt in places you used to love when you were younger? Does this mean that getting older teaches us more about loss than about gain, or even giving?

All of us look back at life. If we didn't, the future would be more uncertain and fearful as it really is. Our greatest act of courage can be embarrassing bravery – it helps conquer our fears. Our greatest fear of all is death yet, our dear departed friends and lovers that have passed on have conquered it. But we have to take many fearful steps in life before we take that one last step in death. We are all guaranteed to get there.

Writing poems and the odd short story is not my greatest challenge on this planet; it is to survive as a human being. To rise with every challenge that life throws at me and still does to this day and always will, until I take my most fearful and uncertain step of all – death. I do not dwell on death and neither do any of us have to. I know in my heart there is absolute continuity for all of us. Is there the possibility of us counting everything and counting for nothing? I really don't know; I really don't.

I was listening to a song on the radio the other day, in the car. It was called *Love is Blind*. As many people in this parish know, eight or nine years ago, I fell in love with a woman. She had this great thick mane of long dark hair, like in Patrick Kavanagh's *Raglan Road*. She had mysterious eyes: I like mystery in a woman. Unfortunately, I fell in love with her and she fell in love with my pocket. Life is too short for me to tell my story of my relationship with her. Suffice it to say, I was duped, with the result that my personal savings were almost entirely wiped out. I never came back from it financially and I don't believe I ever will. I don't do the lotto anymore. When I think of how hard I worked for my life savings, if I met her now, I would not ask for my money; I would ask how could you be so heartless to do what you did to another human being, who loved you so strong and helped you so much.

Perhaps love can be a cold stone nesting in a warm fire with its flame reaching out to heal but cannot reach a dying wound – a wound, perhaps, that can never be closed. Life is backwards but we must all move forwards. Times, I couldn't care. I hear those ghost bush voices. They are not the voices of holy song from a choir, perhaps forgotten and maybe, times, remembered, or maybe just passing through the barrels of bloodletting from our past.

We might as well try and enjoy the journey. For some, it's never enough and others, it's too much. Look out and try and catch whatever is left from a dying star, and test it against your flesh for light. No matter how strong faith is, fear and doubt will test it to its core, weaken it if they can and, in some cases, sadly destroy. This is why we must persevere and be strong. This, of course, does not work for everyone. Poetry will never be soccer, or movies, or music, or rock, or hip hop. But we do it because our heads burn with inspiration, not to mention torment. I would love to see my poems reach a wider audience. In time, some of them will get out to the wider circle. I may be around for it to happen and I may not.

I want to thank all the people for their kindness and their support for my first launch in 2015, just two years ago. My friends in the art world told me that the people of the parish of Ballymoe were wonderful. Of course they are, and they always were.

Prelude

Oh, the weeds of over indulgence,
Tolling in the dangers of ignorance:
A sad and polluted world
That no longer makes any sense,
Still rocking to the bitter dance of thuggery and intolerance.
Oh, they said, there would be better days ahead;
Oh, but better days are dead.
Outside, our doors there are pools of tears,
Our past soaked in blood and fear.
Oh, the withered flowers of yesteryear.
Earthquakes are getting louder and floods are on the rise.
Slavery's camouflage and fear in the future's eyes.
The skeletal imagery, bloodless and in disguise:
From hanging in haysheds to promiscuity
In paid-for, burning beds,
And threadless hearts of effort
Hanging by its beating threads.

Our homeless, our addicts, our old and the shame inside our heads.
Truth can be lies and lies can be truth.
From our oldest bones to our very challenged youth,
Still worried and awake from the night before,
Struggling to keep debt and vampires from the door.
Keep down the middle classes and feed the scoundrel and the hoor.
In desert mirrors and tears that taste like salt,
The shark out there is all our own fault.
It lies at the bottom of bins, they say
And then, the scavengers come out to play,
Through the cold winds of January
To the licking tongue of flowery May.
From the titterings of the clown
To the teasing of the baby's cry,
Those who thought they were too important to die
Had to be found out by the Grim Reaper's eye.
And if we all have to leave now for tomorrow,
A dark world and our hearts dark with sorrow,
We pushed and fought in Troy

And now we must push out our pram,
The burning bush and the bleeding ram.
The fiddlers are now in total denial.

The afterlife goes up on trial.
The clowns refrigerate their smile.
They randomly test and fire nuclear missiles into space.
The sight of starving children and their each forgotten face –
Another threatened cross for the human race.
It's here we tie up all the money games.
It's here we feel the falling flames.
Isn't it a pity how we cripple each other's hearts?
And isn't it a pity, our understanding
Of each other is so apart?
I stagger from life to life in the sorrow of the night
And still borrow from yesterday those words:
Life would see us alright.
But here, we are stranded in its vice.
If we do not wish to drink it up,

Then its guilt, coming face to face from our chipped cup,
In the bushes, the rushes and the hedge,
And the length and breadth of the ocean's edge,
And all that torment and torture
Between every human wedge.
Run, rabbit, run and run like a hoor.
Don't let them fool us into thinking
The human dance is pure.
Blizzards will blow and skies will feed us freezing rain
If we don't protect what it is that still remains.

Do you think we can tell Heaven from Hell?
Dark grey clouds from pouring rain?
Hunger and heartbreak from pain?
And do we keep going around again and again?
De we live in places where the dinosaurs died?
Do we live in a world where equality is denied?
Are we forever running a race we'll
Never win, with no one by our side?
There are no more safe places for the world to hide.
We are hanging in the balance of an immoral, all-out world war,

With a whispering of forgiveness and salvation on that other star.
Will we die in places where the dragons fell?
Do you think we can tell Heaven from Hell?

Foreword

You are lying in your bed and it's time to get up. Get up to face the world. Your heart is walloping inside your chest, your palms are sweaty and you have this desperate anxiety pit in your stomach. You've hardly slept a wink. Your body feels completely drained: almost like, as if, the brain has been completely drained of emotions. You feel nothing. Your body feels numb. You're the dead person walking and indeed, there are nights you go to bed and wish you didn't wake up at all. You throw the blankets off yourself and sit out on the bedside. The struggle now is to pull the curtains over and look out at the day. That's the last thing you want to face: be it sunny or rain, you find it overwhelming and you think to yourself, 'I'm not the person I used to be. What is happening to me at all, at all?'

Desperation quietly inside you, so many frustrating silences inside you: depression, despair, obsessiveness, panic attacks. Nothing much to say. Intrusive thoughts, some of them quite unpleasant, quite uncomfortable. In your stomach, knots of tension choking up your chest. The feelings we don't want to talk about, emotions we are unable to share. Looking out the window, you say to yourself, 'Well, have I to go out there today?'

To put on your clothes is a challenge – never mind, to go out there and work. All the things you enjoyed, you no longer enjoy. You'd rather forget all about the world and life and stay in bed, smoke excessively, drink too much to numb the pain, amphetamines and tranquilisers, whatever. Anything for a clear picture, just for a while, even if it's only for a while. Sadly, for some, the human suffering becomes too much: they no longer belong upon the shore.

They no longer belong upon the shore; emotionally crushed they close the door. I'm not asking for self-pity for people who are feeling this way or sadly, through deep emotional suffocation, can see no other way out. I do not expect you, who have never been there, to understand. I ask for compassion and love and support, for people as they, whose lives are in the doldrums.

There must be no judgement or criticism. We have been long enough in the dark, in the whole wide world. This supposedly Mother Universe that gurus tell us takes care of all of us. You alone can do it but you can't do it alone and you can't. Pull up your socks. Shake yourself out of it. Come on and get on with it. Well, it doesn't work that way. How does a cheerful person – a parent, a child, a brother or sister – go from loving, to giving up trying to hold down a job and socialise with people? A person who is the life and soul of the party and then, hang themselves in the hayshed or take an overdose. Why do they take this action? Why do they want to withdraw entirely from life, their people, their friends, the world, their work, why, why, why? Why do some and many young girls try and model themselves on slim famous models and actresses? They don't know these people; they don't know their world. How can they when they don't have the window to look into their minds?

How many happy people are there, whose happiness has had to change and how many times in our lifetime, does a lifetime seem so strange? I'm trying my best to make sense of it all. Some of it, I will; some of it, never. I gave up being judgemental over thirty years ago. I have enough baggage in my own work, my past, my present and my future. Who claims to have everything? Who claims to be burden free, trouble free, worry free? I'm looking around myself in my own glass world. I will strive and work and write to destigmatise mental illness, people suffering with mental illness and people struggling to cope with responsibility, and women giving birth to and rearing children, and not getting enough support.

Everybody down here on this dark green Earth needs support. We need the Niall Breslins, the Cusack brothers and Noel Lennon, as well as others. Don't ever be afraid to talk; don't be afraid of the steps you walk. Don't be afraid of the power of love or how others see you, or what they're thinking. We're all being busy being born, busy dying, busy worrying and working, busy abusing, busy at war, busy starving, and busy struggling. Busy, busy, busy.

There are a half a million of us out there that we know about and, most likely, another half a million more that don't come forward because of fear and stigma and, God help us, ignorance. So, where do we go from here? We go to love, to therapists, to doctors, to parents, teachers, friends etc. Any place but an early grave. This same grave that takes so many of our beautiful young people. And young people are beautiful. Where am I today? Half-ways content and fantastic peace of mind. I am with you all the way. I don't hate; I don't get lonely and I don't get angry. Never let the sun go down on your hatred or your anger; it will eat you away. Depression is an illness of the mind and body, a cancer of the soul. Let's support one another and defeat it.

I want all of you, whether you are troubled or not, to stay in contact with God. God is our creator and friend. He gave us this beautiful, mysterious world; we have nothing whatsoever to fear from God. Religion has got God all wrong. Pray and ask a loving God who will never stop loving us. He made us, didn't he? Never feel abandoned by him. God is love and hope.

Prologue

Mother and I were sitting in the kitchen after watching *Prime Time*. She was getting ready for bed. She turned to me and said, after the TV was switched off, 'Do you not think it's a bit daft to be writing poetry and stories?'

'No, Mother,' I said, 'It's fully daft to be doing what I'm doing. It's the fire inside my head that drives me, Mother: the highs and lows, the light and the dark, the sun, the thunder and lightning, nature's bright beauty and cruelty beyond belief, running rivers and silvery streams, depression and nightmarish dreams. Isolation of the soul and sounds of Patrick Kavanagh's wink and nudge conversations. It's the borderline of madness, Mother.'

'You're not mad,' she says, 'just talented. Each one to their own,' she says, 'It's a nice hobby and nice passion,' she goes on to say. 'I would never ask someone to stop from doing something they like doing, except smoking and drinking. They're very bad habits,' she says.

Well, I don't drink and I've given up the fags, so she's quite happy in Heaven. Michael would never have dreamed of smoking in front of her, would he? I didn't think so either. God is supposed to have made man out of his own image but, the human element is weak.

I'm sitting here in the kitchen at about four o'clock in the morning. I go to bed when everybody else is getting up: reading, listening to music, writing when possible. Did God make himself out of the black man of Africa, the brown man of south-central America, the Mexican, the red Indians of north America, the Eskimo up north, the Chinese, the Jap, Korean or the aboriginal in the Bush of Australia? Which image? I wonder. I'm sure someone will come up with an intelligent answer: perhaps that there is no body to God. God is not man and he is not a body. Christ was. Maybe someone will give that type of an answer. I don't know; I really don't.

I am now wondering about the word, eternity – infinity; no beginning, no end. Sounds more like a word of punishment than it does of

xv

Paradise. I know it would be terrible to be left here forever. My God, thank you for taking us out of an almost very difficult situation. So, obviously death does give some hope. Science never really said there was no God. They tell us all about coming in on a Big Bang and, if things on this planet of ours (this seriously threatened planet) continue the way they are going, we will all go out on an even bigger bang.

Every day, my mood and my faith is tested – every damn day. But Mother and Michael have sent me an invitation that a sinner cannot refuse.

Contents

Bluesy Ballymoe

Tall he is and dressed in black.
Tall she is and wearing slacks.
The perfect images of a priest.
Says he'll be our saviour.
Says we are our own disease.
Weaving St Patrick's crozier over all our heads,
From the maidens at our crossroads
And the rooms of our burning beds.
Delilah is like a snake
When she strikes out her tongue:
A bitch with crocodile tears
And a tormented sun.
She feels the heat upon her face
But the rest of us are in a different place.

The president is dishing out the drugs
To keep us all smiling
And from being bitten by the bug.
Finn McCool's heart is racing.
You can see him up and down the corridor, pacing.
Tears up a piece of earth and throws it out to sea,
And says he has left puzzled chances for you and me.
Mother Teresa will be friends of everyone,
From Calcutta to Ballymun.
She will bring with her a healing
To stop the rot of our bad feelings.
Take us through a tunnel where Christ gives all a smile,
An expression that says
The struggle was worthwhile.
Widow Rattigan is stuck in a feeling of fright.
Her husband's passing is her delight
But, she is left to fear the ghosts of betrayal,

More than damp muddy places that used to be her jail.
They have sent a clairvoyant in to chase out Caspar, the ghost,
But Casper swears he's here long enough to hang on to his post.

What tomorrow will bring, she doesn't know,
As she gazes out tonight at bluesy Ballymoe
And remarks, it's the end
Of innocence in dreams,
Broken in the paths of which we walk upon, it seems.
The lady newsreader holds a prayer book to her heart.
She knows so much of a world that, merciless and dark,
Her voice shows no expression of pain or hurt.
Void of emotion but, with a crucifix pinned to her skirt.
She sees no wonder in good or bad things;
She sees no wonder in anything.
She speaks about the man of peace
Whose life was about to burst.
Fell into his enemy's arms and died of thirst.
The wicked messenger has delivered all the bills.
War, she says, will never be over
and from here on in, it will be all uphill.

But the spider's cobweb is out there hanging. Still,
Everybody thinks it's going to snow.
I'm looking out my window at bluesy Ballymoe.
Jack the Ripper, he's wearing slippers
And a mind that leaks venom.
Other places being ransacked for the loot
And chimney man is looking up after taking down the soot.
The farmers are looking for money, which seems to be their God.
Maybe we should bring Abraham back and get him to strike his
    rod.
Burn a ram or two in the bushes.

Lucifer is splitting timber for the fire.
There are many people he has won over to admire.
He can be fascinating and he can be dull
But he likes to get inside everybody's skull.
We are left with our guilt and our sin
But, don't let Lucifer catch us again
Because he will be coming around again.

Wear the picture of Mother Mary and keep it together with a
    pin.
We all make promises we never keep.
Lucifer never gets tired; he never sleeps.
Lady Di is bringing flowers and food to the sick and poor.
The Minister for Behaviour is giving out about every waster and
    fool.
Robin Hood is sleeping with a nymph and puts away his arrow
    and bow,
As I look sideways at bluesy Ballymoe.

Casanova and his partner are out the fields, holding hands.
St Peter is trying to cover up his baldness by putting over a few
    hair strands.
The dentist is pulling teeth from all the cranks in town.
Better, he says, not to have them going around wearing a frown.
Einstein is at the party, weighing up a sum;
Wondering who is and isn't a bum,
While his false teeth fall out from chewing gum.
And lovely Rita and her mate are wondering if they should get
    hitched.
For her, I feel afraid: she thinks she might be ditched.
Cher and Madonna are at the alter receiving the toast.
Their toy boys are keeping post, singing, 'I am a material girl,
And this is a material world'.
The hardy boys are on the trail of missing loot.
They are looking to form a band;

They are searching for a flute.
The director's cut says, no more shoots.
He's put on the life support machine:
He's been told his head has to come clean.
All his characters are locked up for what they're supposed to
    know,
As me and my Nissan Note drive through bluesy Ballymoe.

Sigmund Freud is holding an umbrella in the rain.
He talks to all the abused ones about savagery and pain.
Hurt is his heart, he tries to conceal.
If there was a way out of this, the world, he could make a deal.
He says, they tied a knot tighter to the squeal.
And the sad truth is, those hurts may never heal,
Those wayward ones, who should be all lined in death row,
While I go to buy the newspaper in bluesy Ballymoe.

The messenger comes round at midnight
And takes names of everyone.
They leave down their frothy pints and know
That they've just been done.
The barman stares, with a face as red as beetroot.
Don't be too hard on us, he cries.
Oh, says the messenger, you're all going to be skulled up the
    shute.
They are all growing beards for the festival,
That is, if their faces can hold out.

They're talking about a dancing carnival
For the ladies and their gentlemen, and every other lager lout.
They will poison the air with coloured words and phrases
While my dear friend, St Dympna, sits and sings her praises.
Well, by God, says the director, did you see such a show?
As I head off smoking, to bluesy Ballymoe.

The beautician's clinic is filled with transvestites
Coming to confess a so-called mess.

Cuchulain has just togged out with the band.
He's excited; he's just won a grand.
His biggest fear now is that he'll be ridiculed into shaving,
For a date with Queen Maeve, who has lately started raving.
Throw their bodies together and let damnation be as one.
Find them a little cottage, the other side of the sun.
And castigate Queen Maeve's bull, who is constantly on the run.
The fortune-telling lady throws her leg across a man's crossbar
    bike.
Says, today is hers, the future can go and take a hike.
She brings all her clients to where the pied piper used to play his
    tune.
Get prepared, everybody, she says, the futures facing ruin.
Throws her crystal ball into the air
And lets it drop hard to the ground.
The foundation we're all upon is not so sound.
Her husband, notorious for telling blue jokes,
But he only tells them when he's drinking with the blokes.
The poet, Paddy Kavanagh, is having a whiskey, as usual, in the
    tavern.
This is the light of Heaven, he says, as he watches its orangey-red
    glow.
The poet, Paddy Kavanagh and I, recite tonight in bluesy
    Ballymoe.

The parson is hired to clean up the messy church,
Cool off the rats and places where mice lurch.
The servant boy says he's thick and too abrupt.
Have we other weapons to deal with institutions that are
    corrupt?
The parson stops and takes off his hat,
Says to the server boy, I'll have none of your chat.

Faces the furnace to die before its flames.
Now, says the servant boy, not all things in life are tame.
Tells the congress, there is too much to know,
As I run out of tobacco in bluesy Ballymoe.

It was very early dawn.
I woke up refreshed and saw the vision of St John.
He flew off before me to a place called Galilee
And played poker with his friends, beside the Dead Sea.
St Croan puts in an appearance, with a notebook in his hand.
He's being drawing circles up and down the sand.
He's going to help the parish priest say Mass tomorrow.
Such excitement has never been seen before in bluesy Ballymoe.

In comes the newsreader, Brian Dobson with Coco Chanel.
Spike Milligan has just come back
To tell us, before we die, be sure to get ill.
I'm sure, while Spike was here, he had his fill.
All the prophets of doom want to come back for the crack.
Take a hurley in their hands and give the sliothar a crack.
They say they have changed their attitude about all their
    doomed outlook.
Life, you know, is bigger than any written book.
They claim they'll settle anywhere, like an unsettled fart:
The brothel or the ale house, or maybe the local mart.
St Patrick likes rap music and wants to open up a dance hall in
    Toreen,
And bring out every blond and blaggard, from every backward
    boreen.
Eamon Ceannt is back to take life nice and slow;
To have a few jars with his poet friend from bluesy Ballymoe,

Leonard Cohen is behind the curtain,
Singing the Halleluiah song.

Bob Dylan's in the basement, ranting about all that's gone
     wrong.
Me, times I feel so isolated, I don't belong.
And they say that Phil the Flooter wears his wife's thongs.
Phil is bit like a cartoon from long ago,
As I pay the bar lady for tobacco in bluesy Ballymoe.

Lady Godiva takes off all her clothes
And rides the horses back bare.
You could say she was wearing nothing but her hair.
Martin Luther King is in there with the years,
Fighting racism and choking, choking back the tears.
He spoke softly to the world that he had a dream;
The bastards shot him dead in fear of his dream.
Bill Clinton is coming to Guilka, to play a round of golf, maybe
     shoot a duck
And hope that a good round will change his fortune and his luck.
Van Morrison is taking the train in Belfast's Sandy Row.
He's been asked to play a concert in bluesy Ballymoe.

More on the tuppeny whistle and some, the sixpenny drum,
Hoping that all the gurus will come.
Nero has stopped fiddling but Rome still seems to burn.
Rumour has it that Lazarus will return.
The Minister is riding a Harley-Davidson motorbike;
Sits comfortably in his seat,
Depresses the whole country by taxing their fleet.
The failed beautician leaves the country with a double chin.
The old ones talk about the young ones living in sin.
Now that I'm finished, I'm wondering where do I begin.
The joker is getting excited but the thief stays perfectly calm.
Trees are bending in the storm, as if begging for alms.
If you don't already know, there's a place called bluesy Ballymoe.

For all who have suffered on this Earth, they have closed down
  Hell.
For exactly how long, no one can tell.
There's a little beast inside me that wants to lose control.
But there's conscience and guilt, for the good of my soul.
The sixties generation have come back to ban the bomb.
I don't know where they're going or where they all come from.
It's all too late, too many in the tomb.
Leonard Cohen and I have a pint together in the O2.
I told him I come from bluesy Ballymoe.
He takes off his hat and puts it over his heart.
We agree that both of us were writers of the dark:
All the promises that don't get laid;
All the swinging, wild and loose words that get said.

Kitty O'Shea is wrapped around her lover.
They know in their heads, the gallant race is over.
Everyone get down; everyone take cover.
Every drunk in the ashes, rise up and get sober.
In the public house, where I'm planning my escape,
One drunk said, we came from God;
Another, from the ape.
I tell both of them to take it easy,
Take things slow.
The bubbly blond is almost reduced to tears,
Runs out the backdoor with her hands upon her ears.
The comic swinging madly says, life is one big farce,
As he pokes through the tabloids
For a picture of Kim Kardashian's arse.

Doc Holiday is playing poker in the local saloon.
He's playing and blowing up balloon.
In this world, he says, there is only one goddam room,
As his mistress circles him with her broom.

The Father, Son and Holy Ghost have lost their train tickets for
    the coast
And they're given water pistols to protect the post.
Winston Churchill is making a frightful comeback
To tell us that it's ok not to be ok
And to forget the things that slip away.
Damn sod and rotten on the bloody black dog,
Like a bleakness in the frozen frost, a bleakness in the fog.
All that we were and all that we are
Are just thoughts inside of us, near and afar.
And within our skin of wisdom
We're all followers of a star.
As another rattled rhyme goes on show,
Bozo the Clown is coming to perform in bluesy Ballymoe.

Macho Man takes a hanky out of his pocket,
Dries a tear as his eyes roll around their sockets.
We are all moments and living lines as we go.
What nicer could there be than a pint in bluesy Ballymoe?
Dictators are screaming through the microphone.
Musicians are blowing down the cities through their saxophones.
Suddenly, countries find themselves at war, themselves alone,
Trying to clean up their consciences, until their gladness comes
    to pass
And their sorrow and sadness will eternally last.
Sit on a cornflake that floats in my milky bowl.
Sit on wisdom till my mind and body grow old and cold.
Our hours of agony will be the proof of all our souls,
And then we'll both get quietly merry, in bluesy Ballymoe.
And nobody will have to feel faint, when they make Father
    Flanagan a saint.
So, get you to hell out of here, all of you who do not know,
There is a special little spec on this planet, called Bluesy
    Ballymoe

Different Journeys

I pity our poor young ones who have to leave their homes –
Leave their homely firesides that used to warm their hearts and
 bones –
As they board the bus or train, whether it is in open sunshine or
 pouring rain.
I pity our poor young ones who feel abandoned and betrayed.
The savagery of loneliness and the sadness so delayed.
Everybody knows, they'll never change the game
And still, froth and boast at the mouth, without shame,

Their old folks, with tears and blood,
Worked in bog and field and made ridges out of mud.
It took me back to many memories of my own mother,
Waving you goodbye and crying on your shoulder.
It was like someone nested in her heart and broke it,
As she would painfully watch us all go;
As her world and dreams hurt her so slow,

Pictures from the internet, the smart phone and the iPad,
And look up from Australia, to talk to Mum and Dad.
The tall ships and the fast planes have drained the air alive
And sent our young ones to another shore, to thrive.
Left stranded with sorrow in their eyes,
Our children of the Earth, our children of the skies.

Some go on the batter, more on a binge,
The dirty rusted needle and the syringe.
The little mischief angel, to sooth the pain inside
And the opportunist ladies living from their hide.
There may be a glimmer in the mirror, to put away your mask
But you'll still have to be someone, just in case they ask.

I pity all our young ones, into wonder they are forced to stare
Away from their loved ones and a country that couldn't care.

I pity our poor homeless, as they live upon the streets:
So hungry and so perished;
So malnourished and so uncherished.
I pity our pour young ones who struggle with control.
Forced to stare the eyes of immigration or the soul-destroying
      dole.
What we need today, we may still want tomorrow.
Out of the valleys of lies and sorrow,
That slow creeping silence of despair;
That feeling of emptiness in the poisoned air.

Revolution is not quite warm yet:
Still stained in the morals of regret.
The counted countless chickens sprawling across the yard
And the jagged edge of the cockerel's combe keeping guard.
Red, their coloured-language of anger and rage.
The cartoonist drawing characters for the stage.
Here comes the blind politician, looking for a vote;
Kissing babies and their mothers thinking him a dote.
As he rattles out false promises from the pocket of his long black
      coat,
His mask, his smile and grin,
His crooked mouth and his pointed chin,
And in the end, it's they who will always win.

The bog and field has lost its tongue –
Silenced by the absence of the young.
The voices that once said, we would all prosper –
The voices would be prophetic and shrill,
And the great outpouring of the love and neighbourly good will.
I pity our poor young ones online and unprotected.

I pity all our ageing folk, forced to live alone,
Malnourished and neglected.

I pity our rural pensioners, abandoned and isolated.
Everything behind them has melted.
The home help comes and goes again,
As does the frost and snow and rain,
And a pill to sedate and numb the pain.
I pity all our married couples, who have obeyed both law and
    rule,
And see their little children, hungry, off to school.
I pity all our young ones who look back in memories and tears.
Hope that things bet better for their children, in the coming
    years.

Will they still be the product of ships and planes and trains:
The drainage of our life blood;
The drainage of young brains.
But our dawn may one day need them like the sun.
All our children of the deserts will, in their bare feet, run.

Short is their youth, until a newer youth comes along.
They can sit down with the Pecker Dunne,
Hear him fiddle or sing a song
And talk about all the good times gone.
This is not meant to be a sad poem;
It's just all different journeys, of us all going home.
Where they meet their heartbeat at the door
And feel their chains rattle on the floor.
This bitter sweet unknown will be no more.

In the Very Deepest of the Night

In the very deepest of the night,
Her body of threads took her into flight,
Swooped about the sharpened stars,
The Milky Way and the earthly wars,
Wing of feathers soaked in rain,
A mouthful of sorrow and pain.
Never be afraid to close one's eyes:
New knowledge wears no disguise,
While wisdom will always rise.
In the forest, the straw soldiers sigh
At the slanted look in their killer's eyes.
Someone who lives is someone who definitely dies.

Before the new, tattered morning of dread,
Her two wings loosely spread.
There's a handsome figure of a stranger.
It's no Joseph in the manger.
It's just a thought blown out of all proportion;
Blown out by the depth of a dreamer's notion.
The sad attitude that feels forced to carry on,
Through the bars of Earth's lonely song.
We get bad news before good news,
Without getting any news at all
And our pens receive warrior reviews,
And no one cares who takes the fall.

Other eyes stung in sunlight;
Her hair stiff in frost.
Her smile, an angled vision through window light;
Her thoughts in the great territory, lost.
Who is kind enough to be pure?
Who is terrified of failure?

Our bony ideas and our greed,
Hanging from the mantelpiece of need.
Toothless are the cities:
War torn and the onlookers' pity.
You know, God, they say we are all the same.
Who is toothless? Who has shame?
Who is shoeless? Who is lame?
Does she come out of the ashes for fame?
Does the ignorance inside have to be tamed?

In the lingering wilderness of self-doubt,
Hell's kitchens never burn out.
Let us now think of all of them
Before wearing the painted smug grin.
Cheers in their beers, their sin and their gin.
The last thing we want is a pen.
A scribe, scribbling verse and mortal sin.
She cries out from under her wings.
Her whispers are spoken with honesty through her gap teeth.
Her wild mane and her eternal promise and focus of spring.
Through her lungs, the whole world breathes,
Like babies, through their soft gums they teethe.
Look at all the beer guts spilling their madness on the wires of
     their nuts.
I may, one day, get carried by her wing and get tied up by her
     hair,

While the sufferers can do nothing more than stare.
My twin vision sees through the mist so clear:
Heaven was never so far, never so near.
An invasion of a certain kind of peace
That can only be achieved when the bloodshed shall cease.
Childhood widows riddled with bullets of steel;
What's the worst thing that a child can be made feel?

The drift of memory being rained upon,
The child's dreams lost and the clown's face gone.
Not many are smirking in the shadows anymore:
They are being exposed like a crack in the door.
A faint illusion of the woman's wings on show.
We've all being going all our lives, just to go,
Then get scared and wishing years to slow.
The figure of cathedrals in their dust.
The wasters of desire, of flesh and lust.
Mysteries' madness seems to know no end.
Yesterday is no place to begin.
Shrapnel of our own decay are on our plates.
Whatever is the meaningless rage and hate;
Why we allow our heads to fall into such a sorrowful state?
We must not have journey with her and her feathers.
Loss and doom carves out their features.
Scraped the voodoo doll with its pins in every creature.

Desperate thoughts we're forced to think:
The future on abortion's brink.
A soft and fractured verse
Of Christ's spoken tongue.
Suffer all you little children who are oh, so young.
That black dog's line is moving on down.
Chased away all the snowflake smiles.
That house of cards holding out for all the clowns:
An inch, a yard, a crucified crooked mile.

Vibration's verbal pulse roars like waterfalls:
The distance between hanging on and letting go.
She learns to ignore the whinging, self-pity call
And flies the length and breadth of where she has to go.
Her emotions reacting to drowned out craves.
Her breath warm across the mouths of every hungry grave,
Or, be it the swift dancers on the greatest wave.

The frozen gun can still kill with a cheat's face.
The new finders' restless in their own place.
The light of the star and the slaughtered lamb.
Creeping voices being heard from the valleys of the damned.

If we're in the dark, do we get scared
From unknown places to the place we all were reared?
Do we form an opinion of the unknown,
'Till we rest in our nests of philosophy overgrown?
There must be a turning of the earth
To mark our arrival for death.
Suffering is not as painful now
As how it used to be, from behind the plough.
Pushing the earth against the forces of our phoney aggressor,
Our burned-out wisdom and challenges against our own
     oppressor.
In the very deepest of the night,
Her wings of flight disappear
And in the very deepest of our night,
So too will be our battle with the years.

Hey, Brother Michael

Hey, brother Michael, I've wrote you a poem
About a tired, old, worn world that's gone sick and gone wrong.
I wish I could say, it was coming nicely along
But the foundation we're all standing on, is not very strong –
It's as weak as the strength that's in all of our bones.
And nobody down here is any longer safe in their homes.
The fight is fixed and it is do or screw.
Where the vulnerable are crucified and the rich, they are few;
Old pensioners are robbed, battered and bruised.
Women are still used and children abused.
There is nothing down here that would make you feel amused:
Its heart is wounded and its morals confused.
Millionaires' withered-looking faces from Botox.
Paedophiles, protected in the confessional box.

The dealers try to have us thinking, it is black or it's white.
But we all know, in our naked day, it has peculiar shades of grey.
It's dripping blood at its paw that's naked and raw
And innocence stands frozen before its corruptible claw;
You are quite welcome to join them, if you are fast on the draw.
They have the power today that has these big guys clinging on,
But tomorrow could see all of it gone,
As many have fallen down that road before;
As greed locked them all out, the other side of the door.

In a world where courage is befuddled
And truth and honesty are muddied and medalled,
It rides on the thin-edge sword of justice
But don't expect any.
For those who feel they belong to the few
And those who are condemned to be the many –
Many without love and teeth, robbed and victimised,

And people with mental health issues are stigmatised.
Alcohol and drug addiction,
Thuggery, dishonesty and mental and physical afflictions.
The young ones search, so desperate for the truth,
While the older one's sip on pints and shorts and decry youth.
A world that is crushed and its people oppressed.
Where the happy are few and the many depressed.

Times, you cried because your body was worn.
More times, you cried because your soul was torn.
We all know, we can't stay here forever.
I thank God for the beautiful years God gave us all together.
Those loving memories I have of you
And Mother are stitched into our hearts –
Nothing in this world could tear it apart.
Tell me, brother Michael, what time is it in Heaven?
Down here it's Hell and a quarter to eleven.

Life can be of wrongs and rot and rust
But we all must continue with faith and trust.
Our longings come from the cold of our souls
And everything in life that negativity holds.
All the rivers down here are trying to bleed into one,
But it's never going to happen, until history is undone.

God, have mercy on men who treat their women rough
And God, have pity on those who have barely enough.
Nights can be long and days can be lonely;
I think of you and Mother, you and Mother only.
They say that times are a-changing but I don't think they ever
    will –
We will always have clammy-handed foosters in the till.
A world where the bottom line is survival and greed,
And a few crumbs for the many in need.

I've seen you in the sunshine of the garden of wounded flowers,
And I've seen you perished in the fields of a thousand broken
    hours.
You never once complained of the hand of cards you were dealt.
And we all talked to each other about how we felt.
I could see the grey clouds of your cover
Being smothered beneath your skies
And I could see it freezing, right behind your eyes.
Hey, brother Michael, say hello to our loving mother,
To Father and to Big Lall too,
And all the great people of this parish
Who have travelled with you.

In Ten Years' Time

In ten years' time, we'll all be living out of each other's minds.
In ten years' time, our humanity will still be blind.
In ten years' time, we'll still be drinking bottles of wine.
In ten years' time, we will still be victims, counted on the line.
In ten years' time, our poor will be still stretched to the last.
In ten years' time, it will be no better than the past.

Fanatics and killers coming out from the falling ruins and rubble
    of a bomb blast.
In ten years' time, there will still be drunken yells,
Very little peace and paradise but plenty of Hell.
In ten years' time, they'll still vote those into the Dáil
And in ten years' time, it could all fall.
In ten years' time, the churches might have to crawl –
Too many cracks to clean up it all.

In ten years' time, we will still blow each other's minds most
    bitterly
In our desperation to be free.
In ten years' time, we may no longer know how to pray.
In ten years' time, we might have lost the purpose of our own
    say.
In ten years' time, clouds will still be grey
And the pendulum of our broken hours sway.

In ten years' time, people may not feel free to smile:
Sense of humour may have gone out of style.
In ten years' time, children may not play with toys
And in ten years' time, the inner child may be longing for joy.
In ten years' time, the heart may not get time to breathe or
    pause
And violence or wars won't need a cause.

In ten years' time, we may all have to wear camouflage.
In ten years' time, we may turn our backs on the ones that age
And their loneliness be scribbled into history's page.
In ten years' time, there will still be no cure for anger or rage.
In ten years' time, we may be nobody or someone else.
In ten years' time, we could be dust upon a shelf.
In ten years' time, flesh will still roll like burning smoke.
In ten years' time, hunger will still eat and rot and choke;
Still ugly and still without a face.

In ten years' time, we could be all living out of a case.
In ten years' time, there will still be murder and rape;
All the poor unfortunates trying to escape.
In ten years' time, their colour will still not be ours.
There will still be prisoners of the tower.
In ten years' time, life still won't give an inch
And in ten years' time, many of our people will still feel the
        pinch.
In ten years' time, we may not feel we're very alive:
Quietly, desperately, clinging on to survive.
In ten years' time, there will still be skies of sorrow, mist and
        rain.
Our sense of humanity gone down the drain
And strong painkillers to numb the pain.
In ten years' time, they may not ask you if you hurt,
Or ask you if you love or regret.
Their painted smiles and grins behind all that's cute,
You'd want to give them your two fingers and stick it up their
        roots.

In ten years' time, we may still have the sun,
Rabbits digging holes and territory ruled by the gun,
And we feel, no longer, the bond with the Holy One.

In ten years' time, there may be still religion and silly sermons,
And plenty to cover up the vermin.

In ten years' time, the pollution will still be in the air.
We must not be afraid to show our lovely planet we care.
In ten years' time, there will still be tears
Because short we breathe and heights we fear.
In ten years' time, we'll still be taken for a ride
And then they'll scurry off and hide.

Their bulging pockets and their seen-it-all eyes;
This mouth full of word and their bucket full of lies.
In ten years' time, they will still date and hate
And in ten years, the frozen ones will meet their fate.
Ten years from now, there may be no now:
The moon may make way for the sacred cow.

In ten years' time, we'll still get drunk,
Wobbling around like a dying heart
Beside the huge tree trunk.
Snoring and whoring, burping
And fighting and farting lie a skunk.
In ten years' time, we may have to leave: leave someone;
Forget the past and forget the sun.

In ten years' time, the whorehouses
Will be full of nakedness and despair.
And in ten years' time, they'll be places
You'll have to leave without your hair.
In ten years' time, there will still be underground crime.
The pimps still win and men won't mind.
The world will still be in conflict
And the laws of survival will be strict.

In ten years' time, happiness will still be as big an illusion as ever.
Heaven may not be a paradise forever.
Gamblers will still gamble and gamble with other people's
     hearts.
Places where time and money wink in the dark.
In ten years' time, we'll all be still be sad and depressed:
The puffs, the pansies, the paedos and the undressed.

In ten years' time, old joy may be forever lost;
We will have too many wires of the head crossed.
In ten years' time, there will be no such thing as shame.
God will always be on trial, always the one to blame.
In ten years' time, there may be no more lyrics or music:
They will have murdered it by something acid and tragic.
Yesterday may become the new tomorrow
And tomorrow, a hiding place for the now – the broken now.
Forget yesterday, they all say,
Yet it's the engine room of how we are today.

In ten years' time, people will still have to cue up in line
And the sick still waiting on trolleys, be it of body or mind.
In ten years' time, humanity will need a moral boost
But money and power will still rule the roost.
There will be still drug abuse and child abuse and women
     abused;
Places where the body is interfered with and the mind used.
Tomorrow, tomorrow may be ten years' time,
Injecting into our living blood lines.

Gaunt and worn bodies will still be standing on Slavery Hill
And girls will be running to the pharmacy for the next-day pill.
They say, don't dream of yesterday;
Oh joy, you have been hurt all along the way.
In ten years' time, they still see the soul.

People warming their hands against the cold.
People in pain, looking for euthanasia and being in control.

Factories will still pollute
And the aggressor will still loot.
Victims and their perpetrators in hot pursuit.
In ten years' time, there will still be anger and rage.
Still clowns and killers dancing on the same stage.
In ten years' time, will we breathe in fresh air?

Will we honestly show nature and humanity care?
For 'tis short we live and high we fly,
Smiles we laugh and tears we cry.
Watching the incoming and outgoing tide;
Stay balanced on the stormiest wave.
Postpone the undertaker from digging their early grave.
Will we still believe that only Christ will save?

In ten years' time, will they believe Jesus died on the cross?
Will wires get crossed and truth get lost?
Will they believe in his existence at all?
Will his birthplace be for children so small?
Will they believe in churches or sermons at all?
Will the world still be that great big jungle for us all?

We'll still feed our cats and give the dogs their bones,
While middle aged are afraid of ending up in nursing homes:
A sense of insecurity that threatens
Their little thrones.
People will probably take their little pets for a walk.
Computers and iPads that will talk.

Our history books will still unfold
Stories of starvation and wars of new and old.
We will still be new colours until we turn grey

Against the limits of survival for each and every day.
In ten years' time, will the underprivileged still be looking at life
    through bars?
And men still working hard on high stools, in hotels and bars?

In ten years' time, will you be loved, will you be kissed?
In ten years' time, will you have thrown it all away
Because you lost the meaning, the truth and the way?
In ten years' time, will my poems set the world on fire?
Will we still want to look like the person we admire?

In ten years' time, will we still kneel down to pray before bed,
Or will it have become a vacancy in our heads?
No such thing as prayer books or Rosary beads;
Will they search for poor St Anthony anymore?
Will there be searchers on the other side of the dark door?

In ten years' time, will our hearts still beat love and blood,
And will nature purify the little, new-born bud?
Will Voodoo be sticking pins in that voodoo doll?
Will our most vulnerable still be made to beg and crawl.
Our God be left out in the cold to freeze
But will be warmed again by a gentle breeze.

The strippers will want to wear their mother's clothes
And leave the boys scratching from the dose.
Christmases and New Year's will probably pass off with plenty of
    food and beer,
But it won't have the same good conscience and cheer.
They may come and go as just another day,
And New Year's Day will be new but, only for a day.

In ten years' time, we could be all doing fine,
Loving each other, drinking champagne and wine
But only when we've left our shell behind.

Gaza

This thick billow of smoke and ash rises up into the sky
And you can smell the poison in the air.
Innocent woman and children slaughtered in despair.
Violence and ugliness everywhere.
Bodies picked out of rubble and falling houses of stone.
In their misery, you can find yourself very much alone.
Suffer the little children that come unto me.
Well, suffering and bloodshed is exactly what we see.
How could God, you might say, let it go this far?
But it was his free will he gave to man, under his immortal star.

They are our fathers and mothers and sisters and brothers too,
    you know,
Why let it come to distance of hatred?
Is anything in life any longer sacred?
The breaking down of the distance between bloodshed and grief.
So many packed together like sardines in a can,
And the world watches but it doesn't seem to give a damn.
All those beautiful people dead and dressed out in tinfoil.
Someone bombs the Holy Wall
And against the wall of terror, you can hear the people call.
Their voices cracked and broken from poverty, graveyard stuff,

As they are chased down their own land hard, hot and rough.
Sought out in their tanned skin,
The very vastness of their very existence, bloody and thin.
Life begins red, raw at its tooth and at its claw,
Bores holes into the imagination of whatever law.
The joy of the child is crushed to death in the playground.
The voice of innocence drowns.
Their holy bodies, now of rubble and ash,
Feels like you need to get pissed or even smoke hash.

Be on some side of any other side, where there is no cross or
    nails.
Cry, stop, inside your broken spirit, until the world fails.
And now, another country seems to want to play the game of
    sanctions,
While the vulnerable are up the junction.

The unholy mists of mayhem spread across every newspaper
    page,
And frantic anger draws on guns and games of death and rage.
Locked away by centuries of hatred and hurt,
Their eyes wild and their knuckles blurt
The tidal flow of their blood-fuelled, red veins;
Their prisoners and their bodies dressed in chains.
Blessed is the gift of everybody's child
That froze their very smile.
Hezbollah, Hamas, Jihad and Jew,
Their majestic words of truth and foam,
Through thick smoke, came through.
But it's only wisdom dressed in camouflage;
A scattering of orphanages on war's blood-stained stage.
They will kill you if you are disabled.
They will kill a child in a cradle.

Most of the time, I'm at pains with my mind.
It's been dragging me down into a bottomless line.
I feel the confusion because the plot is thick.
I feel the pollution; my stomach churns to get sick.
If I could shoot myself out to the missiles in the air.
What good would I be, if I didn't care?
If tomorrow gave me a present that I didn't have to see;
Turn my back to pretend I didn't see and didn't want to be.
Be the armchair viewer of my screen
But my heart rises up to take me
Through passengers in their eyes.

Rockets and tanks burst open and pump explosion 'neath the
  skies.
Great red balls of molten poison taking the light from their eyes.
Take my sedatives and retire to bed.
Keep the secrets of Heaven's mystery locked inside my head
While my children of Jesus are being riddled with lead,
Lost and spread afar, scatterings
Of bone and blood, being dead.
Their lives are no more than tea leaves of a clairvoyant's cup.
Sometimes love may be not quite enough.
Behind all enemy lines lay crushed waste
And now it's this crushed waste that may be all they've left to
  taste.
They can't give up their ghosts because they are still perishing.
All of God's little children, we should be cherishing.

Moment by Moment

In the moment, I am me, a journey that, maybe, was meant to
    be;
Lungs to breathe and eyes to see.
Big wide fields of grass,
A horse, a cow and an ass.
In the moment, I am an illusion
Brought around from death by spiritual delusion.
There are ageing bones that rattle in the dust.
A swinging bedroom door with hinges rust.
It's not in the moment I've a mountain to climb,
Or in thoughts, the thoughts I must leave behind,
And in this moment, that's no more than an illusion,
A fixed fight, a rowdy drunken occasion ...
If the clowns take off all their masks,
Is there a better and newer way behind all our tasks?
On the verge of coldness, they stand
With viscous remarks no one will ever understand.
In the harshness of their shiver –
Victims carried away, on downstream by a river –
What way is a moment supposed to feel
When truth cannot save the complex, turning wheel,
Or whatever way the mind moments reel?
It's an ugly black ghost that has come again to steal
The moments that make up me and you and them
And in moments, some will be never here again.
Jump the moment into the piggy bank
Where the coins don't shine and the air is rank,
Or uncertainty has preyed upon its watery banks.
Draw conclusions or go out and get tanked.
Knowledge is something philosophers teach
But the depth of it seems to be forever out of reach.
Another non-believer sees no sense to truth.

They can only chew on common sense with their teeth.
No tongue will ever be strong enough to sweat;
No words are too strong to repeat.
We are trying to and begging to,
To know what's beyond belief.
The fast, black night and the thief,
And the Holy Messenger too:
Other illusional moments of me and you.

In the dilapidated chapels, there are broken voices
That cannot speak, that don't have choices.
The fancy necktie and suit.
The flickers who couldn't give a hoot.
The bastards and the scoundrels
That went off with all the loot.
In this very moment, look at them now,
Forced to stand behind their earth and plough.
In this moment, the heart can beat through a dark hour.
In any moment, the heart may only have an hour.
In any moment or street, there is a shoeless foot.
In a hungry or anxious soul, a burning gut.
The summer roses are fading and dangling for winter's claws.
Clamped in coldness, our flesh pushed out by our jaws.
In my youthful moments, I wanted to be a protest singer.
In these moments, I am a poet and a bell ringer.
Foolish for anyone to think that life is fair:
The blood-letting earth and the poisoned fare.
Tell me, Eagle, where am I flying when I'm aching and half dying?
For moments now, the sands of time are running out.
Oh, depression; oh, darkness, I felt so lost,
Worse than any burning bridge I'd ever crossed.
The barbwire feel of your touch –
Perhaps, perhaps some of us worry too much.
In moments of delusion and battered scars,
Puppet soldiers look through their prison bars.

Give them an iron hat and some clothes,
And tell them which way the wind blows.
In solitary confine that have yet to be peeled,
The body of holy blood and the corpse of steel.
In some precious building, they rape and still cheat,
Throw the clown's frown down and eat human meat.
From one another's cup, they drink our blood
And in these moments, are these creatures caked in mud?
Come out of that thistle;
It's from your rural mouth you whistle.
In the moments that make up hours that are quiet,
You'll hear some kind of hammering, kept out of sight.
I'm still fighting with myself for the common good:
It swells my veins; it burns my blood.

Random Thoughts

All that I'm doing is all that I've done;
What I was winning is long won.
Capturing mysteries with their bodies of wine,
Their masks and the cobwebs of their minds.
The white energy along their lines.

The midnight breaks open its wheels of wisdom;
The heavens and their hearts, a new kingdom.
With their eyes lit in the punched air night,
Those crazy ideas, they hold so tight.
Shoot the wick of the undertaker's lamp light;

It was first lit, to light up the GPO
And its heat was felt by a satellite, hovering over Ballymoe.
Eyes are wide and blurred and sore,
Reminiscing all their days of yore:
Sweet and merciful, slim and sleek,
Burning the temptation pages of the meek
And building with turf mould, to make a reek.
The love junkies behind the arse of a pen,
They cried out for pity in their underwear of sin.
Told not to worry and go back to their Guinness and gin.

Lightly these creatures in love trip along.
The sky always hears the bird's song.
These twisted wreckages point an arrow to the end,
While my nursed broken heart is on the mend.
I hear there are strangers among us we must cast out.
Violence happens in the audience of self-doubt.
Burning rainbow bridges and trimming ghostly hedges:

Those we struggle to tame,
And those who struggle themselves to be tamed.
Wicked and weary and all times lame,
The sky is sharpened but the day is dull.
The refugees living out of the icon of their skulls.
Madness can be lonely, pushing its way through.
Innocent faces can turn raw and blue.

The homeless children say their world is of lead.
You can't even take memories with you when you're dead.
We are afraid to face our fears,
Afraid to be seen openly shedding tears.
I am so fragile now, being stretched and naked in my bones.
On this wintry night, I struggle with words for a poem.
But the messenger, I will not send her home.

Our bodies are fastened by wisps of clay,
Stripped by window light and the day.
Cry before every protest words we say –
Rome is burning, again and the rivers burst their banks.
All our victories are stained with guilt,
Like we're boiling in a hot spit.
The mirror of our tomorrow will stare back at today,
If ever the future gets to stay.

Show me a bullet that doesn't bleed.
Show me hunger that doesn't have need.
Show me a place where pigs go to feed.
Bowie is bleeding from his black star;
Do we really know what we really are?

No place for justice, only room for thieves,
Bombers and creatures eating away at dead leaves.
No round of wisdom, no round of relief.
Stutterers finding difficulty with faith and belief.

Suffer the little children that have come out of you all,
In hardship and shelter, in some dingy hall,
Some prophets with their wasted words' wasted call.

I don't have anything for myself anymore;
I feel like two rusty, half-swinging doors.
I can't hear the sound, just the croak:
The gut wrenching of children so mild and meek.
I see them ice cold and behind barbed wire.
I see them in clubs and pubs, getting higher and higher.

I see through a stained glass, the cracked mirrors of reason,
And I'm disappearing again, with some cold, changing season.
My limbs feel as though they are being torn apart
As I gaze into the ugliness of a dark heart.

The phantom of the opera seems to own the whole stage,
While David fights Goliath for a space they call rage.
I can only look and I can only stare at helplessness, held in
    helpless air –
Almost as bad as being back to the days of my despair,
And all other torment that dwelt beneath my grey hair.

I will cheer up in my hours of choice,
When my ears become deaf to all the world's noise.
I will walk again in fields, all wet with rain.
All green, the grass will come again.

Mother Wisdom

She danced a vision in my eyes.
She stood on the point of a needle
And slipped through its eye.
She had fallen from the heavens;
She was borrowed from the skies.
There were wheels of emptiness
Dancing in my mind.
But I took to song
And I took to rhyme.
There is no nothingness in Time.
She comes upon me with great
Force, stronger than any woman.
She feels inside herself. I'm human
In your heart, she says, there is sadness.
In your head; there is a running madness.
I asked her if I could hold her in my arms.
In your world, she says, there are so many storms.
I asked which way the wind blows.
She said, Well, really only God knows.
It is out of love that everyone is here
And out of love, they will disappear.
O Holy Mother, have me warm forever, unto thee
And not a grave in the depths of the sea.

Getting Lost

The hypnotic splutters of dust
Lay waste upon the earth:
Faded, jaded, back into rust.
The hinges creak and crack,
For everyone, there is no turning back.
No more than just one last hour in the sack.

The only things left alive are breathing.
Other ones, left stranded and bleeding.
The misfits in the corner cannot have their word;
They've just come from a hard and broken world.
What does it matter, when you can wine and dine,
And be the distractors of our very own minds?

I saw them buried and saw them dug up;
Saw them falling deeply out of love.
I don't see the ending of this abandoned and broken waste.
As for talking, they don't seem to have any taste.
They swear drunken words underneath lights dim and low.
Nobody left to worship; no heroes left to follow.

They'll give you ammunition and stones,
And some tablet to take that weakens our bones.
I've almost grown out entirely from your own dust.
My gurus tell me to never say, must.
My ex-girlfriend's taught me never to trust.
Jarring our heads, this ignorant delusion
That love and happiness is our ultimate solution.

They are not dead but, their handkerchiefs are loosely hanging in
  the air.
They search for empathy – must be somewhere out there.

My eyes are wide open, wide awake.
The dreadful day will soon have to break.
I've seen them all standing in a smoky haze
And I know now, they will all vanish in the days.

Flung down, I am with lots of sorrows and twists.
I've slipped in on the doorsteps of a mist.
I'll probably ride out with snakes in my fists
And anger and chains tattooed across my wrists.
Don't keep no dinner for me, Love; I'll be eating out in the cold,
Preparing to sharpen the edges of my soul.

As everybody knows, there are wars to be fought and won and
    lost
But nobody seems to care, at what cost.
Maybe our lives have been busy at getting lost.

To Chapel

I went to the chapel today
To chase all my demons away.
Got down on my knees to pray.
I see my reflection wearing the suit of clay.
My hours going from moment to moment;
How pathetic is my light of day?
There is no need for greed or hunger;
No need for fear.

Bring this new awakening out of some kind of closet tears.
I can see where its hanging from; it's been there for years.
The ghosts of my doom throw shadows to the womb
Because it's not really what dying does;
It's not someplace that memory goes;
There is no breath from dying rivers' veins.
Heaven holds no place for ball or chains
But is sometimes lost in greed to reign.

Its many hurt victims in the rain,
Pressed against Liberation's false promise at the new dawn.
Love and Freedom sold off as a pawn.
Scattering of orphans, like statues, wear
Some kind of expression that wants to swear.
Oh, bring me on home from being alone.
Every time her lips kiss mine,
I turn to stone.
Back into the chapel I go.
I hate it fast; I like it slow.

Guilka

My heart's in Guilka, under the woodland air,
Standing away, so timid, so gentle, so fair,
With the vulnerable rabbit and the run of the hare.

Winds are chasing sounds of blue.
Black laughter from the heathery bog.
The scowl of the cat, the bark of the dog,
The swish of the fish and the leap of the frog.

By the island river of the beautiful white swan
With its ever-flowing waters, forever moving on.
My heart's in Guilka where the bluebells blaze
And the livestock graze.

My heart's in Guilka, among tall standing trees
With the wind rubbing music through all of their leaves:
Nature's orchestra, like a sweet violin.
Away from the panic, you feel safely gathered in.

Dandelions dance and buttercups bloom.
In this world, I can still find room.
Take a flower and hold it in my hand:
Soft as a child's bare footstep in the sand.

Many of God's creatures are there to be found.
So much of life is lived underground:
So many secrets that will never be found.

My heart's in Guilka where the dawn begins to crack.
I can feel its pressure from the heat of my sack.
Take a drink of purity from its spring well,
Guarded by the blackthorn bush and the weeds that swell.

For a fiery tongue, it can fuel its fill;
For it lies at the bottom of the sloping hill.
My heart's in Guilka, from midnight till noon,
With its apple orchard and its abandoned ruin.

Those scattered voices and those missing bones
Of broken spirits among falling stones.
The painted sketches on a ghostly sheet.
The midnight cries of the fox, through its hungry teeth.

My heart will always be in Guilka, through poetry and song.
It will always be there, even when the last light's gone.

Dreams

Patches of uncertainty that have been stitched
And all that was certain, that was ditched.
Those colourful voices blown in the wind,
Through the passages of God, may send
Whatever comes up from the cradle:
Those who are not and those who are disabled.
Put my diplomatic hat on and say, I'm angry;
Put my cartoon face on and say, I'm still angry.

It's ironic but it's nice
To know I have a choice:
To plunge myself into the ocean
And pretend these sanctities are just a notion.
A game of phoney guesses
And a nod of, maybe, no's and yeses.
How precious human life is;
How important is justice.
Life, in our creative imagination,
Has exploded inside us.
Froth and foam from our destination

Darkens our clouded night.
Foot has walked
Instead of mouth having talked,
Down the drainpipe of despair.
Broken down beneath the upper hair,
This great warzone economy,
This blank eternity

With its family broken in its flesh frame
And toy guns that spark its childish game.
Taking a look at your own face

Is like looking at the wide-open spaces.
It spreads like eagle's wings,
Floats and falls on everything,
Dampens the reality of dreams –
Keep us stitched up at the seams.

One Inch of Hope

The sun is light and the wind is too,
And all the faces here are new,
And shades of sight are coming into view.
The trapdoor of innocence broken wide,
Battling from the inside,
To get answers of truth from the outside.
Temptation's pages fall scribbled to the floor,
Between the sheets of Heaven and the valley of the whore.
Pressed against unlimited sin
And the face never lived in.
No place to start, no compassion to begin.
All our old men, burying their past in their pints;
All our young ones, facing an uncertain future, smoking joints.
I need an umbrella to shut out the rain
And someone's affection to shut out the pain.
Hard times would come and hard times would go:
We learned to live with the hardship and learned to let it go.
All those words I write and rhyme –
All God's, and guardians of the mind.
We have many inches of rope;
We have one inch of hope.
Cowardice leads to silence;
Bullying leads to violence.
Our shamed religion on its lame duck spin.
You'd swear that darkness was the greatest force against the
     eye.
Or, we should pretend not to hear the force of a child's cry?
See the ghosts sitting on Slavery Hill
And the many graves to be filled.
I will scream obscenities under this sacred sky.
I will go as far as the diamond in its eye.

Homeless Beggars

I can see rivers run through their veins,
A sense of hopelessness running through their brains:
A chemical form to numb the pain.
Flung down, the watery stain of rain.
Laughter that once filled field and bog
Have now become coloured, like the distant black frog.
The world is hungry and the world is hard.
The poor have traded in their every word.
I see them, sometimes, through the vacuum of my eyes.
I can almost touch their lowliness, underneath those sacred
    skies.
Their hard faces show the journey they've come.
Worthless and demeaning words, like vagrant and bum.
Their loved ones now are but a distant touch,
The pain of coping, having been too much.

My Beautiful Bird

I set you high,
To float the space
And feel the sky,
Through the rounding
Diamond of your eye.
Your wings caress the air;
Glide so magnificently and fair.

If they gave me wings and other things,
I'd float with you forever more,
Just like we did in the days of yore.
And in your heart, your flight will hold
The mystery of light, which may yet unfold
And be the saving salvation of our souls.

For food, be it not our every need.
In chase and haste, we grab and greed
And blame the other for sowing infectious seeds.
Sprout out underneath our thirsty feet;
Flung down the vagrant and the hobo on the street.

Oh Bird, I see the sunset start to die
Through the storm in my mirror's eye.
O Spirits that are now once lost and gone.
Oh, such joy, floating bird, to hear your song.
While rivers run and mountains roar,
I watch you glide and watch you soar.
There is no time and there is no end,
Just me and you, bird, and everyone to begin again.

Pain on Pain

You cruised above the rivers of rain.
You disappeared from your whips of pain.
You didn't have to knock on Heaven's door:
You were met by angels at the shore.
Away you go, you Guilka boy
With your little Christmas toy –
A world that offered you very little joy.

Your world burst its banks of its river bed.
So glad to rise from being dead.
What went wrong with your beautiful mind
Through rolling wounds of the sands of time?
I know the world treated you like a stigmatised stranger
Because you were never them, or he, or it, or her –

Your bed was hard and so was the manger.
There was time when you were so young in the world's eyes
And you were never one to surrender to disguise.
You ran with the wind and you came home with the corn –
The human joy at your being born.
Little did the world know, you would be young to wear your
    crown of thorns.

All those many screaming broken hours;
The long time you suffered in the tower;
Your lonely garden that offered you no flowers.
They advertised the Hereafter as a place of fear.
Before your journey and your struggle, you shed a tear.
Those ugly instrumental forces of yesteryear.

Having to live out our lives of thought and time.
Our steel cross melting in the flames of rhyme.

Lost was your young laughter of the bogs,
Of swimming, tadpoles and leaping frogs.
The hairy heather, drenched in sod
And voices of nature's beauty, speak from the breath of God.

Your sacred holy innocence bare –
At such wonder and glory, you stare.
Your eyes rise steps above the thoughts that tormented you.
Many a time, the hayfield screamed out your name.
In honey-coloured sun, you had to struggle with the days, in vain.
They never did offer you any truth or laughter.
Your pockets had no map to take you to your shelter.

Your warm skin has broken into sweat
And the world you leave behind, without raw regret.
Theirs is a sweetness of healing colours of the sunset,
We little kids would wrestle and tumble into weariness,
Many little grains of childish happiness.
Our early morning fields, covered with God's web.
Watching the swans' great white necks
And the rivers freshly flow and ebb.

Times, we were almost savagery in our existence.
Your Guardian Angel has gone the full distance.
She would never leave you, never deceive you.
It's not the wind or the word that keeps you up.
Love alone, may not always be enough
But if we are planning to turn into gold,
Then it's a poor friend of the soul.

We are all kings and queens but only in story.
You got to pick primroses from the ditch,
Burst the arse of your trousers and mother have it stitched.
Still, the memories of your native home, while feeling far away,
The blossoms bloom and the bluebells groom

And their presence takes you into beauty's way.
A boy with lots of dreams like any other man.
The broad world out there, you could not make your stand.

This internal turmoil on the far side of your brain.
Your shorn locks, your weeds of pain.
Where to begin, where to stop and pause
And where not to start?
Heaven holds the blood of all our hearts.
We took him out from his dying sweat
And sometimes, I wonder if his spirit is all in us yet.

Oh, what by-road you came from as a boy,
To see the face of the wide-open space
That gave you so much joy.
Sure, you had to toil the doors of doom
But the blossoms of your heart were forever in bloom.
We turned our heads and faced the rising sun.
We were no worse, no better than anyone.

When they tied you to that electric chair,
They shaved your dreams and they cut your hair.
To question it, well, who would dare?
In a world that couldn't give a tinker's curse or care,
In other lands, you dreamed you could have been,

Stories to tell and so much wonder to be seen.
Oh Lord, when you show us all your jewels in the skies,
There will be candles burning inside all our eyes.
To wander out from a certain type of suffering
And stand naked before your many offerings.
And his heart leaped with great joy,
When you showed him the fields he played in as a boy.

Your Guilka pilgrim sitting by the old spring well.
One last drink before they ring the bell.
Another battle between the saints and demons of Heaven and
  Hell.
You've had your Hell and now, your wings scan across all
  eternity.
You died on a warm summer's day,
When the world was in bloom
And now, the heavens open up
To unlock your eternal room.

Our Father, Who Art in Guilka and Now Art in Heaven

Mornings, I can hear your Sweet Afton cough,
Feeding oats to sheep, around a trough.
Rubbing your dishevelled beard upon our faces.
Taking us to fairs and other places.
Minding cattle, like you mind mice.
It would be all right, you'd say, don't think twice.
Cattle scuttering up against shop windows.
Dogs barking and scabby cats with their meow.

Hot summer days, sweltering in the sun,
Running the hunt beside you, with your gun,
Your hat turned sideways on your head.
And God bless the living, and God rest the dead
And the love of God, be good to us all
Through spring, winter, summer or fall.

You were the emperor and the king,
And we, your bodies held by strings.
Old Mother Hen, racing across the yard,
Half blind, fully foolish. Rex, the dog, keeping guard
Even though there were never going to be
Any Apaches raiding the fort.

Guilka was too primitive, too quiet;
We only existed in our own sight
But Father, we lived and we learned,
And nothing of the world, behind our backs, burned.
There was always the swing and the sway,
And the half-light of our memories of the everyday;

A longing we could run to but not from – never from.
There were always lost gatherings of grain in the corn.
Father, your mad little tearaways
Playing games of hide and seek
And you, swearing over a hay knife,
Cutting a bench from the rick.

You lived on your wits and times, by tricks.
Fights were fought and marriages fixed.
Strong whiffs of frothy pints of Guinness,
Its wisdom rolling down each side of your mouth.
For everything brought and sold, a witness
Huddled under a doorway, looking out.

Your slanted hat and your ass and cart
Rolling home, long before the days of the mart.
A bundle of chops in one arm and an ashplant in the other,
Ready for the frying pan, to be cooked by Mother.
Mother packing lunches, getting us ready for school –
She might as well be packing a mule.
Chasing butterflies with you, Father,
And you, watching us swimming with the swans.

The measure of every hour of every day now gone.
Picking potatoes and poreens in the still
Of a half-light, half-cold October's day.
Togged out after coming home from school
To dance above the clay.
Knee deep with you in the bog,
Fiddling in the drains for tadpoles and frogs.
Our hands, outstretched, catching turf sods
And the faint sun lapping it up with the gods.

I can remember the colours of our breath,
From bog to field and your undying love for the Earth.

Moments in our minds that twist and faint
Become new to tomorrow's new coat of paint.
Listening to the waters gush in the boys' cracked banks.
Saying the Rosary with you and Mother, giving thanks.
That little spec we all were and still are,
Underneath Mother Mary's silvery star,

Washed by the wisdom of the heavens.
Pints of Guinness galore, after Mass, on Sunday at eleven
Bring both sides of the road, with your bike,
Red faced and blotchy skin at closing time;
You are all told to go take a hike.
Sunlit morning meadows speak of an early dew
And the corncrake, they'd be in there somewhere too,
Washing their beaks in the dew-coloured grass.

And you'd say, Willie and Michael, go catch the ass.
There was nothing, Father, like the freedom:
The master of your own kingdom.
You and Mother taught us to milk cows –
And get the shit kicked out of us.
We were all afraid of the cow we called Magpie –
Her swinging, scuttery tail and the demon sitting in her eye.
But we, eventually, got the better of her with your ashplant.
Kick now, you bitch and his voice in a rant.

Every cow we'd sell, would see us weep a little inside:
We little children found it so hard to say goodbye.
Goodbye to a cow of fifteen summers;
I asked my father, are all his animals just a number?
No, he said and his voice slightly broke;
There was a little tear he was trying to choke:
No one likes to see their animals go.
I knew there and then that in our hearts,
We grow fond, too fond to see them part.

But it would be foolish for anyone to think life is fair.
I often thought of the day, Mother and Father would have to go
    into God's care.

The life blood of their children walking up the steps,
John Joe heaped high upon their shoulders,
Big Lall having already walked up his steps.
A chill in the day, getting sharper and colder.
This chapter coming to be very final.
All your children in denial.
The slate grey-coloured rocks
That the waves of want lash against:
Rough and ruffled, and ready for to blast.

Father, I remember you,
When you were much taller than our shoulders
But we had to carry you, nevertheless.
There was wet clay in Killcroan cemetery.
It used to be the month we'd pick potatoes and poreens,
And study geometry.
We all lose to find that we will always lose.
Tell us we have choices; we all can choose.
I am so much like you, Father;
You have given me the reigns to be a leader.

Your body now lying in Kilcroan's big sleep
And the Keys of the Kingdom have been given to you, to keep.

All That We Are

I have feared God right down through the Dark Ages:
Frightened of him in different stages.
Religion's crooked and twisted pages;
The hidden chapters closed like dead eyes.
The beast at the dark gate,
Cloven-hoofed and full of hate.
A promise broken before the colours of the skies.
Oh God, you must have shrieked back away from it all,
Hearing many desperate, fearful human calls.
The hands opened wide before your heart:
Your sacred, healing heart.

The many hot and tortured souls lost
In the eternal burning chaff.
Merciless, their words falling into phoney
Faces that mock and laugh,
Sin having never been photographed.
The puppets and the clowns are hanging around the fire,
Their heads hell-bent on desire.
Must we all rise up from the ashes of decay,
Holding memories of our loved and lost ones
In the hardness of the day?

I've searched through their wisdom, now long out of date
And put my faith before the final date.
Plucked corruption from fear and hate.
Through lovely, green earth, your sheep walk.
Out of pockets of emptiness, I have come
To be the other side of the honey-coloured sun.
Where we are free to love and play and talk,
Our challenging hearts can rise up
To feel mercy strong from the wine of our broken cup.

Flung down, those chapters of perfection and purity,
The smell of roasting flesh and body into all eternity.
Our struggle to survive, our struggle to live
The love from his heart strong enough to give.
To breathe into our nostrils, smelling the stench.
Seeing mercy so far out of reach.
Whispers from the word of lies beckoning.
Our fire-stained string hanging out of our day of reckoning.
Everyone threw stones, got hurt and broke some bones,
Searched through their spiritual poverty from their own homes.

Spoke of love and mercy, despite the flames and smoke.
In the green valleys, many is the good shepherd that got choked.
Feeling cold, they left us with bitterness and regret –
Anger before the open doors of hurt.
The shamed unmarried mother speaks through
The tears of her missing child:
Burn with Original Sin and a God with a frozen smile.
Frozen we came, from the bitter sweetness of our breath,
Our fears and failures, before the chasing dance of death.

Far into each other's eyes, we stared for the truth
Long after the living was abandoned from their youth.
All those withered, threatened bodies separated from the fold,
Like ashes and dust gone through
Their mouth, not of the soul.
Counting our sorrows and a more forgiving attitude.
Shovelling guilt into their bedrooms of stained gratitude.
Lost in the whispers of the parochial tongue,

Love and death will rise up together
Before the face of Satan's burning sun.
What if we fear our heads and fail to climb?
Will the gates of goodness rise with rhyme?

I am standing, feeling threatened in my living skin,
Fighting the preacher's book of words and sin.
The same sin that tore the world apart;
The same threat, there to break
The chord of the human heart.

It's a constant battle to keep clean our minds;
What are we expecting from all of this?
All of eternity, free to live without time?
The breath and the death of the green Earth's kiss.
If we believe in nothing, then nothing will arrive.
This constant battle of the books of prayer to survive.
If we wait for someone, someone unknown could arrive.
And if we don't live and let live,
Then all beautiful and delicate life will die.

If we love each other, then nothing will die.
Forever, we will live and high, we'll fly.
All we touch is maybe all we'll ever be.
All our golden wonders are maybe all we'll see.
Our constant craving of spiritual thirst
Eats into our hunger, makes us feel worse.
The misunderstandings of each other's word.
All the voices that were oppressed, that we should have heard.

A raw awakening that hits you in the face.
A disappearance and another unknown place.
Riddled with uncertainty doubt and fear,
The goodness of the Saviour's breath is very near.
Them and you and me, trying to get each other to agree
Words and works out of our dead oceans
And the shark infested sea.
No date is set, yet, for us to leave.
Behind the word of constant deceit,
A fear of it all is what we perceive.

We must have no inclination of looking back on past mistakes.
Hone in on our thinking conscience so that
No other book will lie or break.

Every healing promise that was drunk from the chalice,
Now trying to find compassion in the moments that make up
    silence.
Poisonous like the serpent feeding on dead sand;
They knew it all because, no one put up their hand.
Now that we know, there must be a closeness,
A passing sadness, an incoming gladness
Torn down from the shorn locks on the cross.
All the wise ones that followed stars and still got lost;
We fell because we believed in every word.
Let's give our needs a chance
In this bitter lonely dance.

Our sad-eyed prophets, with their pressure-cooker grin,
Leaving holy men and women feeling weak in the galleries of sin,
Failed to pick up on the tenderness within.
We cannot be controlled by either word or book.
We must be more than just another fish
Or someone else's hook.

Sometimes, life laughs and sometimes, it hurts
But we must never again go back into the dirt.
I remember a time when they valued with head.
Could get you into Heaven, once pronounced dead.
Had a hotline to God and a safety catch for Hell.
In the spiting flames, you can hear the corpse yell.
How long is tomorrow, before we feel
We've been too long here today?
What direction do you think the pendulum of the soul will sway?
We've searched for balance in places where the vultures feed –
I could have eaten with them but, there was no need.

And now, the purple fluff has changed my eyes:
There is no fear or loneliness I idolise.
In Guilka village, they could not chain me down:
My world was small but at least it went round and round.

The west winds blow, they blow hail and snow,
Swirling around our bodies as we go.
Our bodies held by strings, perished in their frame.
The preacher following the sick and the lame.
One day, they say, the lion will become tame.
Oh, Jesus, I wish I could have walked
Beside you, in peace and love and grace,
Besides looking for you on the cross.

What do you think you gave us when you said your last
    goodbye?
A place of peace and love, where salvation never dies
And judgement, more imagery and fear in one's own eyes.
So how can we walk away from the breath of guilty air,
Not being afraid to show one another we love and care?
We have all had to swim muddy waters they pushed us in,
Through sadness and sorrow and sin.
Time is against us; let's strengthen the things that remain
Because the planet will never again be the same.

Mother Earth

I am a mile and a half from the frozen fog.
I miss my mother, my brother and dog.
I miss their voices in both field and bog;
The hissing sound of the fire, burning logs.
My sadness and my footsteps rise
Much, much more than I realise.
The half-light studying my explosive eyes;
Those little parts of me that keep on dying;
The frantic heartbeat that never gives up trying.
To cling on to memories that make up sadness and loss,
And the shoulders of no surrender, while having to carry my
    cross.

There is a place in all of us, where only flesh and blood shall pass.
Our religion, our buckets of sweat, our sermons, our Mass.
I am stretched across your homes and graves,
That part of us all that yearns to be saved.
The hungry heart for intimacy;
The longing on our cordless tongues,

Blood red, looking for mercy.
I hear the sound of donkey's cartwheels spin fire;
A sound somewhere that takes my loneliness further and higher.
That screech of the hawk as it soars;
Its victim, lifeless and frightened of its last roar.
I see you, Mother, coming in your summer flowery frock
With warm bottles of tea, wrapped in socks.
And Daddy, firing out the turf
And Big Lall tightening up his jocks.

Our voices and language spoke through field and bog, flagger
    and rush,
And our orchestral friends singing sweetly on their bush.
Oh, countryside, you are very short of childhood
But we were the scrapers of the mud,
Everything lived and died in blood.
What is there left for me to see
But memories of us climbing the highest tree,
Turning the green sod over with horse and plough,
Sitting on our stools, milking the cow?

Sometimes, I feel I'm going nowhere
But falling fast and falling home.
Left with memories and a world that couldn't care,
I'm a hermit, a recluse, a rolling stone.
Picked by hardship to the bone,
My mind's eye sees us all in fields
Of fun and tall, yellow-headed oats;
Fields of cattle, sheep, grass and goats.
Everything can seem hopeless, if you let it be that way.
When you can't see inside yourself,
You can't seem to see anywhere else
But I am lucky, in the silent fields of passion's play.

Memories of your rural childhood can become dark
When you've no one beside you to light the spark.
That hunger of the body for another body.
Grief and loss and fear are the enemy.
A world that was once a playground,
What's left to break me now but a silent sound?
The real enemy being abandonment and fear.
That constant struggle with my yesteryear.
If tomorrow's eyes do not blind mine,
Then I'll keep those memories as beauty from the mind.

We are a light that shines and a love so pure.
Many is the day we spent feeling insecure.
Walking through the woods, far from where the world shouts
And our rural evenings, beneath the sky, stretched out.
Let me walk through half-deserted towns and villages.
The slow mutterings coming of age.
My visions of its openness coming towards my mirror's face.
My loved ones decreased and having gone to a better place.

I will not go searching for all my broken nights.
And seemingly, my soul longs to continue to be a beacon of light.
The freezing fog that rubs its stains upon my teeth,
Muzzled by the thinness of the week.
That great scattering of children with their hands outthrown:
Their eternal joy, hunger enough to starve a stone.
Their touching of the branches
Through their sunlit day;
They do not weep or fast but, they work and pray.

If you spend a long time listening,
You may spend a longer time whispering.
The strains are on your sweaty tongue,
The force of raw, running blood and the drum beat of the young.
All orphanages and scatterings now,
All of it thrown to memories of the sacred plough.
The many nights, up watching the calving cow
And many nights, up watching the aggressive sow.

I do not let my footsteps chase anymore;
Just the odd failing this side of the door
And forever, I will cry no more.
Cry at anger, cry at shame, cry at sorrow.
Try today for love and peace of mind.
Cry even harder still tomorrow.

The hanging cobwebs gathered from my many chased hours of
    time.
Was this our word, the launch of a billion human strains,
All tied up in life's hardship chains?
My thoughts are not me, or yours you
But there is a time and a place for us all to come through –
Be it be where the Earth is green, or the sky is blue.

Unrest

A place where the easy chair is brought in from the cold;
It belonged to the bewildered tune of soul.
A picture on the wall where the cheek bones are gaunt.
Places where ghosts travel and ghosts haunt.
Where there are lots of need and want.
It feels so dark now, I can hardly see.
We are pilgrims crossing over the Dead Sea.

These figures are now bent backwards in the wind
To a place where poison and trust begins.
Fresh veins, running poison and blood
Against the backdrop of their neighbourhood.
Out comes the communicator with his vision to halt the ugly
    spree.
He got hit by a hard word coming and was left to be.

Our dying parts within us. If words don't come, we cannot see
Our lifelessness and our gladness that has come to pass.
Sunday morning Hell at Sunday Mass.
I'm sitting on a haystack with my pitch fork.
Its silver sharpness pierces the shadows of the sun.
We're all hearing the song of the meadow lark.

Over fields of blood, the good shepherds grieve
And the starved peasants leave.
Peace of mind must come, cries the old, grey-haired woman
At the half door.
Dust and disaster will lift when we sweep the floor.
And thunder will come on the wheels of fire,
Where our madness will run us into rough desire –

A simple truth into the beating human heart.
Our flags of surrender, circling the mantelpiece made of arch.
Fairy Godmother lights a candle for our dead.
I'm afraid they'll rise, she says, in torment and dread.
Their shell of change hanging by a yellow thread.
Their soul without their shell, hanging by a golden thread.

The children of tomorrow will draw blood
From their fountain of worship,
While in the Dead Sea, men will abandon ship.
There is no worse lie than the one without truth.
No shallower voice, the one that decries youth.

The mad mother with yellow hair
Begs from the clod to heat her fire in the air.
What must I lose, she says, before I am a widow.
The spider gathers its web beneath the window.
Will peace, she says, ever come at all
Behind the secrecy that guards every brick and wall;
Before the deafness of our own false idols call.

Mother, yellow hair, you raised us all to be,
To know and to trust, to feel, to love and to see.
Be by the strength of each other's mortal decay,
A source of wonder in each other's day.

Observations of a Passenger

The youth are pouring healthy
Through a song and a drink.
The old are pouring poverty
Through a nod and a wink.
Wounded both in uncertainty,
Hurt by life and love,
As I hold on to my crucifix
Underneath the skies above.
The laughter is chasing,
The froth and foam racing.
Still wetter dreams are spilling
Like the takeaway chips and grilling.
That restlessness has me feeling
Like wood was made out of stone.
And that anxiety has me reeling
Like flesh planted on bone.
Those voices are breaking down slowly
As my temperature dips lowly.
Tight and formed in the night,
In old and young and in sight,
Not betrayed by words or meanings,
Not lost by rhymes of wonderings.
Shifting themselves into shades
Sharp as a cold razor blade.
That skin, the beauty and poverty
Towards a timeless eternity.

Wondering

Seated in the smug knowledge of knowing
This kind of a hush magic,
Like the day lit by bulbs glowing,
Or a young woman looking shapely and chic.
Before me, there are mountains and frontiers
As I lie in my bed of thought
And change each chapter,
While wrinkling with the passing years
And examine what the traders of life have sold and bought.
Physicality coming from the guts of the body
And emotions repressed under the unconscious mind.
The spirit going back to the beginning of eternity,
The dust never far behind.
Soaked in the running stream of a dream
With the silver moon reflecting
And the frontal wounded form, forever projecting.

Why Me?

The depression is gone
But there is a longing:
A longing not to live on.
Feelings of emptiness
And a dying in the words of my poem.
A shadow loss of my second coming home.

I feel I'm holding snakes in my fists.
My plot is dark and taking too many twists.
I can feel a hammering in my blood,
My face as hard as dried mud.
I feel, at this stage, life's just a run –
Nowhere for it to end, nowhere to begin.

I have no flesh and blood running by my side,
Just lots of dark room but no place to hide.
What did I do to deserve these scars?
I didn't poison the Earth or pollute the stars.
Although I fee higher than the ground,
I feel unwrapped and naked without sound.

It is not always easy for one to look up.
Sometimes, I feel the world is no longer enough.
I see those lonely, quiet, green places
Where I used to play in as a boy.
Little green places that gave me and brother, Michael, so much
    joy.

Places that were so silent and so green:
Such beauty still quiet and unseen.
I carry it in the morning, in my eyes.
I carry it in my heart, under night-time skies.

My God will keep me safe and warm.
My God will take me through this dark journey, this unsettling
    storm.

There were too many things back there for me to come forward:
From the quiet lands of Guilka to a psychiatric ward.
In some ways, it's a pity these things can't last
But who wants to wear scars of the past?
Lying on a straw bed
And all those abusive memories in my tormented head.

I once remember the priest preaching Hell
And fire and death and sin.
I felt choked in my shadow and didn't know where to begin.
He sat stone-faced with his smug grin
And I wondered, what the hell all the fuss?
We can live without our shadow
But our shadow cannot live without us.
Times, my thoughts are so naked I can feel the flame.
Times, I no longer want to be part of life's plan or game.
Looking from within and out through my blinking eyes,
There's a lot of snow on cold mountain, a lot of ice.

Love

I've been there, shortly after I stopped playing with myself,
Half-steamed in the sound of music
With no dust left upon my shelf.
We were early children of the dawn.
We were young and we were born.
The very first time we caressed each other's lips,
Dancing with our hands on each other's hips.

Our bodies sweating under the moon above
And yes, yes, we were both in love.
We felt so small between the stars yet, so large against the sky.
Older than the wind and the mountain's eye.
She and me would race and run together,
Driving in my little Renault Four car.

To the world, we were lovers.
Within each other's hearts, there was
Nothing left to discover.
Yes, there were still wars and tanks and guns
And tasteless dead haunts in their sun
But me and my little girl, Hanna, were in love.
Our young eyes of vision of the heavens above,

Till in the passing of time, it was no longer blood:
I of dust and she of mud.
And now, I'm getting old and poor, Hanna lost
And memories stored inside the head of frost.
I won't complain because I don't feel pain
And Yes, I'd do it all over again.

Lady's Life

She is wild and she is free.
She has carved her degree.
Times, you will see her swim the sea.
Other times, locked into you and me;
Her journey, a complete mystery.
She will kill you if she can
But that is not where she stands.
She wants to tell us all her story
Before the world becomes too violent and too gory.

In the distance, she sees nothing, not even a broken smile
But she has walked many a crucified mile.
She is not a distance put between moments and ourselves.
She will not stand in front of you or behind,
And she listens to the dead and she sees the blind.

She may ask you to stand by the window and suck in the air,
And show you a new tomorrow without despair
And hold your tired feelings in her hair.
Times, she will cross over to change her name
But she never looks for fortune or for fame.
She knows eternal damnation is poison gas.
She can see through both sides of the glass.

The age of life may be coming to an end
But there's no stopping us to begin again.
We are so small and uncertain
Between now and tomorrow
But growth, she says, will come from
New seeds we all must sow.
Psychologists tell us, we can be all happy and full of beans.
She says, no one was born happy or born with a screen.

Suicide, she says, is a quiet silence of deaf desperation:
A very quick ending with a little preparation.
There are many, she says, who take more than they need
And lots of open wounds that still bleed.

We must not lose each other in our freedom
Or reach too high for our kingdom.
Our wisps of pain can be nurtured
And our philosophy become tortured.
A good shag or a spiritual experience –
Forever or for tuppence.
She says, you cannot have trust in humanity,
For it's false and it's blurred,
And to suit themselves, have their own law
And their own word.
People bending backwards to break sacred laws
And the whirlpool of our morals clamped,
Like crocodile jaws.
You can find your real self,
She says, in the beauty of verse
And lose yourself to someone else's curse.

There is a time for oneself and plenty of time for rhyme
But it comes too late for all,
In our bed of dying.
Looking into the open mouth of some black hole.
Looking for some fixed trick for their ladies up the pole.
She will not take you on a journey of the suffering soul,
For suffering is a type of dying –
We must learn to unfold.
The branches of my garden
Hang shadows over the grass.
Although our journey began long ago,
She says, we all have arrived at last.
No yesterday or tomorrow – an imaginary past.

Oh, beautiful woman of the day and of the night,
You do not have to shiver for us all in the cold light.
You can play your trumpet and me, my violin
And we'll do our best to reduce the wages of sin.
She touches the earth, now so suddenly bare.
She cruises above with her angel plans in her hair.
My eyes are bright and my face is red;
I'm alone long enough now to know
What it's like to be dead.
But she still visits me and she
Brings me wine and bread.
She is, forever, in each and every one
And will be there when your problems weigh a ton.
It's me and you, my friends, who are the strangers
But our prisons are safe and in no danger.
She will help us all to find our manger.
Through our wanderings, our steps will always rise,
Allowing us to surrender our disguise.

Gypsy

I went to see the Gypsy,
I was under nobody's care.
I found her in the kitchen
And she had long flowing hair.
I couldn't see her deceitful disguise
But I saw her great, big, green eyes.
Did I come to throw it all away
Because this loner felt astray?

From the corner of my eye, I caught her crystal ball.
Little did I know, she would catch me by mine.
Down that journey of a long-crooked line,
She had those Latin-looks appearance;
She mirrored broken innocence.
Smoke from her candle billowed towards the roof,
Wondering, should magic and humanity have proof?

She took me out into her mystic garden.
I farted and begged her pardon.
Little statue figures dangled from her ceiling.
I could feel part of my insides freezing.
She said, 'William, hey, why don't you sit down beside me here?
I can rid you of all your fears.'
Her black cat was playing with his shadow by the fire;
A slit of light through the window reflects the face of a liar.
She spoke strange words over a deck of cards.
My pulse vibrated and my jaws felt caked hard.
She had this mocking laughter and a voice like a rasp.
She held the poison inside her like a wasp.
She said, 'William, my friend, drink it up.'
I foolishly emptied the cup.

'Your future,' she says, 'is of money, love and dreams'
And I wooed her with my poetry, by a silver running stream.

In her darkened room, where I lay,
I felt naïve and depressed.
She shook my hand and said, goodbye.
I left with my senses all undressed.
God bless my late, loving mother for she warned me to take
    heed
But I didn't understand individual female greed.
I see good and God in every living thing,
The cold of winter, heat of summer,
The fall's falling leaves and the pure breath of spring.

Once, I had promises and power in my day
But the Gypsy took it all away.
The language of beauty doesn't always rhyme.
Nobody knows nobody, no matter how long the time.
Creation is perpetuated out of offspring,
The bodies that walk and talk
Listening to native sing.

O Gypsy, you have turned inwards on your own curse.
Your smile stiffening on your face and worse.
Your children smoking pot and drinking out of control.
Your husband gone to find a warmer soul.
You, having destroyed your own
And betrayed the skin that covered your bone.

I open out my welcoming arms to beauty and to space.
Seeing the world out of my Mammy's tomb with a warm face.
My pockets empty but my head and heart are clear,
And love those many friends that I love so dear.
There are many flaws and regrets out on life's highway.
I wonder will death fall upon her dishonesty.

My Suffering Inside

My suffering inside my head;
I must confess that I feel dead.
She lies beside me and she's awake.
Nothing I want from her – nothing I want to take.
It isn't hard to be there.
Every bit as thin as a rib of hair,
Her victory was complete.
She spreads them across the bridges of sorrow.
I couldn't tell her, there was no tomorrow.

Somewhere between where her and God was born,
She donned the uniform.
It lifted her out of the measure of all scars.
I tried to tell myself, there is no suffering before the stars.
Lots of light; no fence, no door, no gate.
On a higher difference, one could call fate.
She called, reasoning of the head.
I called pause to all who have passed away
In peace, to become dead.

But I have it here, living in one like a soaked slice of bread.
Nobody but she or me can devour me.
Leave me feeling disloyal at the bridge of misery.
Feel her body numb and disloyal
In taste; it's almost like betrayal.
Were you someone who could love me forever?

A poet loner whose shelter went into a shiver.
They have rolled away the stone
That covers the shiny bone.
We held each other for a little while,

To see the gods turn outwards their smile
And my head was once again in turmoil.

The poems of peace, the bitch of dishonour,
Survival and truth within this hour.
All the mad nights being a number in the tower.
Blessed is the name that is brave.
Blessed is the hope that is saved.
I have followed the path very slowly,
My mysteries unknown, hanging lowly.
She baffles me, from the beginning of time.

My poetic vocabulary, she says, is baffling to her mind.
I say, woman, sit beside a cold stone
And say a prayer you can call your own.
I will be always just a moment away,
While you come to term with blood and dust and clay.

Unrequited Love

I felt a victim of the toothless city;
I was trying to lose self-pity –
The side that always seems darker.
Burn out my insides that were her,
The torment that was she,
The internal turmoil that was me
Drenched, only to be dried out.
Get me through emotional self-doubt.

I asked God to take me over to the other side
But he says, it's not time and besides, the river is too wide.
Times, my dreams grow so tall,
I'm afraid I might fall,
Be found out and caught by the balls.
She burned her way into my brain;
Now, I must throw her out through my pockets.
I can hardly stand the strain,
Drunk, with my eyes rolling out of their sockets,

We'll never be the one body, in either mind or thought
And her lover, I'm certainly not.
I neither feel her compassionate or hot.
Once, tried to dance with her with feet of clay
But I almost lost the power of my day.
I felt pressed against Original Sin.
No mental state to start over,
Only a short space to begin again.

A Tribute to Big Lall Tiernan

I can see you, standing in your great frame
And us, as children, playing a children's game.
Hand in hand, you walk us through your land,
Your broad shoulders spreading across the earth.

And you showing us a new born calf,
After its mother's given birth.
Teaching us, always teaching us
The wonders of the joys of life
And telling us that life sometimes can be strife.

Watching us chase butterflies, through summer sun,
In the enchanted meadows of fun.
Sorrow never found its way through you to us.
Life was one big plan, never of fuss.

Cycling into your farm on your bicycle,
With Silvermints for us in your pockets
And us, wild, running round in circles,
Wild out of our sockets.

Thoughts streaming out of our skulls
And you showing us your great big bull.
As the sun poured like honey from the skies,
We wandered together to watch the hare rise

And see the rabbit scurry,
Without your world being in a hurry.
Melting, as children, in your great shadow.
Easing back into the balcony of love through a window

That reflects the images of greatness.
All out of truth and memory and love and fondness.
Watching you and Father on a hot July day –
Your big chest expanding, lifting great forkfuls of hay.

And now, your adopted children must stand underneath the
    sacred sky
And watch you slowly die,
As we repress a hot tear from our eye.
Memory walking down a dark lane.
Emotions feeling hard the pain.
Perhaps, Heaven's gates are opened wide
For your flood of frame to flow home with the tide.

Body Bags

Fallen faces, forced to drag.
Horny soldiers need to shag.
Seems some of them want to go home in a body bag.
The lifting of the child's balloon,
The shadow of oneself, seen in the silver spoon.
The morning passing on to noon.

Our winks awake, our eyelids fallen,
Our tongues, our voices calling.
Unto the slipstream of a dream,
As tightly collected as a funeral ream,
The rifleman walks on solid nails;
The train, on iron rails.

Who rises with the bare-naked flash
Can be a hunter stripped and ripped of his cash.
Across you lay, in harmony in your head
With a dream as heavy as noise and lead.
The curtains are caressed by the butterfly.
Alas! We will:
Nobody's here to stand still.

Berkeley (Tunisia)

We swallow in disbelief. We wallow high grief
At the story of Berkeley in utter disbelief.
Emotional feelings of fear and dread.
Our beautiful youth now dead.
A cry, like a banshee
Before the sacred silent sky,
That the loveliness of our future could die.
Their loved ones watched them
Go through the mirror of God's face:
Another world, a different place.
You – and beautiful and funny like I once was –
Inhaling the perfume of change and adventure.
Our brightest and loveliest of the future.
And why? We may never be sure.
Our mother country has mothered them all in love.
Nothing can touch the mysteries that lay above.
A hard silence sits in the body of God.
The millions of sympathetic handshakes
And the millions of sympathetic nods.
A frozen love that we all, together, share.
A nation on its knees that really cared.
It wasn't drugs or suicide and it wasn't drink
That brought our consciousness out to its brink.
Today, it was Ireland, real and raw.
From Berkeley to Tunisia – the other side of lawless law.
There was no need for imagination behind our pain.
For our lost summer whose skies have burst open with rain.
Our split images seeking distraction.
Our nerves lit for reaction.
God's dance of love and breath.
One does not associate youth and beauty and brightness, with
    death.

We all see love as being young
But we never saw death as being young.
And the longing that it has left on all our tongues
When we feel loss in our hearts,
We also feel the hurts.
We have all little ships and boats in life to sail;
Little dreams and visions, and ambitions that sometimes fail.
Even Creation itself can seem so fragile and frail.
As our weaknesses and our senses rise,
So too, do the tears in all our eyes.
Tasteless can sometimes be sour,
For we know not the minute from the hour.
But we must not allow ourselves to despair:
There is a spiritual force out there that really cares.
Gone now are our lovely young of the holy face
That walked with Christ, in love and peace and grace.

Poems with Streams of Consciousness

I was there when they crucified our Holy Son.
There when they killed with the first bullet, from the first gun.
I was there when they led the lamb to the slaughter house.
There in my house in Guilka,
Setting a trap to catch a mouse.
There when they were shooting pheasant and grouse.
I was there when I fell into a cloud, a dream.
There when I heard the children scream.
There when I thought newness brought with it something real.
There when I thought the world could think and feel.
There for the refusal of the ride on the comic's wheel.
There when they brought the sharks in on the reel.
I was there when the snuffed out poor old J.F.K.
There when the blood became the thickness of the light of day.
There when they shot poor old Martin Luther King.
There when the angels lost their voices and couldn't sing.

There when the sea washed up diamonds on the shore,
Then greed and thuggery and blood, they bore.
There when they raped women in fields and on the sand.
There when they stole innocence from the child's hand.
I was there when they scribbled others blood into the world,
Raped and murdered while saying their word was God's word.
There to hear some of the greatest bullshit I'd ever heard.
There for the licking sickness of the tongue.
For the betrayal we sprouted out to our young.
There for vengeance, without remorse or pity.
There to see that the other side of the glass was always shitty.
There for the unclean thing in the cartoon city.

There when they passed on the buck.
There when they couldn't give a fuck.

I was there when they built it up
Then, under orders, ripped it down.
There for promises from political culprits and clowns.
I was there when they told us we had to hold on.
There when they said, forget the past and move on.
There when they glorified war into music and song.
There for ignorant injustices dished out to the many who are
    wronged.
I was there when they allowed rapists to go free.
There when my river died, before it ever reached the sea.
I was there when The Beatles sang, *Let It Be;*
When I heard the bluffers' sprout, what's to be, will be.
There in slits of light at the highway of death.
I was there to witness our Holy Mother's birth.
I was there to see the filth they brought upon the Earth.
There for the undertaker's curse.
There to listen to writers of pornographic verse.

I was there when they built the railway tracks
Where slave workers were abused – that very sad fact.
I was there when youth thought of reform.
There when the naked were refused to be brought in from the
    storm.
There when shelter was as dry as goodness of the bone.
There for poets of passion and true gods of stone.
There when the sermons became no more than a scribble:
The young and powerful never saw old age and dribble.
I was there when the children were beaten because they were
    unsure.
There to hear them preach,
Masturbation was sinful and impure.
I was there when they classed others as second rate.
There when they couldn't forgive but could continue to hate.
With them who shivered nerves on first date
And now, and rightly so, the bastards must repent.

There when hard cases became pious, just for Lent
And no one seems to know
Exactly how it was all spent.

I was there when they captured the black man and made him a
   slave.
When they abused their women
And overworked bodies into an early grave
Then, when the dust fell from hands and they claimed not all
   could be saved.
I was there when the Heaven's opened and the threat of Hell's
   damnation raved.
There beside the unmarried mothers put to shame.
There when the men didn't have to share any blame –
Free of mortal sin and stain.
There with evil Hitler and Stalin
And their ugly moustaches.
There with the monstrous dealers of heroin, cocaine and hash.
I was there when communist Russia and Lenin roared out, There
   is no God!
There with the mongrel teachers, beating children with a rod.
I dug billions of holes for the lifeless under their sod.
I was low when the whole world went high,
Then lost its face to a blizzard sky.
With all the martyrs with a cause and willing to die.

Then, when they smoked dope,
Listened to every lecture from every pope,
In harmony and understanding
For those who lost their lives by rope.
Beside all the sleaze bags and pissheads
With their corrupt ideas and their adulterous, burning beds.
There when they bombed Nagasaki and Hiroshima.
There to the sound of Leonard Cohen's Halleluiah.

Vietnam's running, frightened children whose bodies were a
    furnace.
There for every ugly war and excommunication that didn't have
    a face.
I was there when they passed laws to murder the unborn baby in
    the womb.

I was with the sixties' generation who marched to ban the bomb.
There with the red man, when they butchered his people and
    stole his land.
There with Live Aid, when the world came together to lend a
    hand.
I'm there with Black Africa, who have a dignity in their poverty.
I'm there with those many who fear the future and the wheels of
    soul's destiny.
I was there with every hippy with flowers in their hair.
They talked of love and freedom but it ended in despair.
I'm there with the sick, the deaf and the blind,
The marginalised who feel neglected and left behind.
There with the many who trawl their lives for peace of mind.
I am there for all visionaries who are mocked, heckled and
    jeered.
I'm there with the mothers of the disappeared.
There through all the centuries of hunger's confused faces.
The strugglers dislocated and the helpless displaced.
The feeble bodies too weak to tie their lace.
There for every pothead and pisshead
Whose brains are wired up to space.

Those who poison their souls with bigotry and racism.
Those who cannot cope and seek shelter under substance and
    escapism.
Those many getting themselves caught on the wrong side of the
    track.
Life can become difficult and feel there is no turning back.

For those who feel abandoned and let down;
For those who wear a streece
And those immersed in a frown.
There with every hooker and hoodlum,
With every flesh saddler and bum,
And the many spiritual thirsts that have yet to come.
The devils that wear Prada and the ladies in stilettoes.
The scab near the headstone and the many syringes in the
    ghettos.
For Master Chance and Mrs Hotpants,
And the circle inside where the whole world dance.
Here to try to heal the families that are broken.
Let the book of taboo and stigmatisation be forever open.

The pauper who failed to realise his dream;
Those scantily clad ass ladies on the scene.
I am there for every hoor and harrier that ever walked and
    talked;
For every boasting Botox that baulked.
For the gentlemen who like a bit of chaff and pulp.
The ladies who like to giggle and like a bit of gulp.
I will bring in the many from the cold:
Every sheep belongs to his master's fold.
I could have saved everybody but the body holds so few.
Sad about the Holocaust and the slaughtered six-million Jews;
A negativity on this planet that seems to only want to bring bad
    news;
The many who will be judged by the chosen few –
Does it really matter, whose first blood we drew?
There with the crusaders and the inquisition.
The civil rights marches who seek your name on a petition.

For every Tom, Dick, Harry and shit,
And those who blow their lives to bits.
For the bleeding hammers and the bloody dicks.

The hungry, thunder and the know-it-all pricks.
For every layabout and lager lout and thug.
For the lot of you pulled out from under the rug.
For those bowing down upon their knees
And others, in adventure with the birds and the bees
And the songs of rejoice, coming through the wind-filled,
    whistling trees.
From Saturday night's debauchery to Sunday morning
    hangovers.
Those with a straight face and those who can't stay sober.
Those who did their best to keep things straight,
Down on all fours, banging outside Heaven's gate.
I am here in a world, more troubled now than it ever was before
But I am a human sacred heart;
I will never close my door.

Poetic Illusions

Benny and Barney Buck are heading out to shoot some duck.
Lately, they've been feeling down on their luck.
George and Georgina have both been put out to grass
But they still keep the faith;
They still go to Mass.
Mick, who has been known as the local dick,
Is fencing himself in, brick by brick.
All the local folk are going to the dance,
Taking something stronger than tea to keep them in a trance.

Tom and Tessa are feeding their sheep and goats
But their recently squeezed jackass has broken into the shed of
    oats.
The village children are peddling bikes without breaks.
Is it true that women in the saddle can sometimes fake?
While Casper, the ghost, bakes a cake.

Depressed farmers are sent for by the beautician,
For shock therapy from the local electrician.
Secrecies are being kept behind closed doors
And leave the tunes to the troubadours.

Rita and Rodney are practicing foreplay in the haystack.
Romeo comes home moaning about being let off, having got the
    sack.
Democracy, they tell me, is gone down the drain.
Behind freedom, there is always some kind of pain.
Nothing passes this way without strain.

The bachelor bum that's drinking rum,
Pinches a young one in the bum.
Every man in this world must do their shift.

It's their male sexual fantasies
That make them change their drift.

They are bringing the hunchback of Notre Dame
To clear up waiting lists,
While the pied piper plays to human rats with snakes in their
    fists.
The Father, Son and the Holy Ghost
Are badly stranded on the shore.
They're waiting for a ship driven by Pussy Galore.

Empty bachelors, stranded without teeth or love,
Are all online dating underneath the sweating moon above.
The sharks are all been fished out by sailors holding flowers.
The lovely Nuala Carey promises sunshine with flowers.
We can all be happy and holy, at least for an hour.

The disco girls are plucking their eyebrows,
Their boyfriends sweaty from milking cows.
The timeless machines have been kept so unclean.
Booze-fuelled voices of the night, so obscene.
We've all got the time to leave
But not the time to stay.
The sun may come up tomorrow,
For tomorrow to become today
And prisoners will be let out to make some hay.

Let us all be and be in eternal places.
The ex-Lord Mayor of London is caught pulling faces.
The Houses of Parliament have gone to Brussels, fishing for the
    day.
The Oireachtas committee has nothing more to say.
Peasants are searching for gold in a ditch.
Vladimir Putin and Lady Gaga are planning on getting hitched.

The Devil and the son of God are playing chess.
The souls of the Earth are wearing bullet-proof vests.
It's not certain who wins.
You can hear all the non-believers hiss and boo –
I told you so and I told you too.
The phantom of the opera shouts, he has nothing left to lose,
But warns us all, in our bedrooms, to be careful whom we
    choose.

God bless you and God bless them,
All things without, all things within.
And now, we must grab the future by its squeezed nettle,
Bring back the art of conversation
And boil the kettle.
The deserts are painted and all the lawns are mown.
I think I'll be belting my way back home.

Frightened Heart/Thought

Your frightened heart seems to bask in duality.
There must be a level of consciousness,
No key in the I, self, me for all eternity,
Our inner bully being the source of our own unhappiness.
The birds do not need to sow and reap:
Everything is there for them in abundance, in great heap.

The I in me, out of insecurity and bare survival,
Has poisoned the meaning of God's arrival.
His arrival in us is not, in any one of us, without essence.
Alignment speaks of one's love for one another;
Non-alignment sees us struggle with evil.

They named him, Satan and gave him enough power
To be as strong and as connected to us all:
The danger of faith coming to fall;
The imagery illusion of a fiery held call.
God's own children punished by the evil force, Satan.
A powerful idea, in our fearful minds,
That religion cannot make its own plan.
Nor, beside religion, do we ever have to stand.

Our lifelessness and our sins posted
Against the wreckage of consciences.
Disharmony and our own failure to be at oneness.
How imagery can steal the thunder of our mourning selves.
Our body cells finding higher purposes;
Our eyes just see what our mind sees.
You are not religion and you never were religion.
You are there for us in all perfect regions.
How strongly we allow ourselves to be tricked by thought –
Our imagery of this non-productive nought.

We claw towards the heavens, beyond the universe
But, that does not mean we are a size.
Every cell lives in the moment, never in the outworn.
The outworn is out of date and punctured beyond repair.
Awareness has been feeding us lots of nourishment;
Religion, in God's eyes, a source of punishment.

At shrines and holy places, they await the miracles of God.
They stand with doubted faith with them
And if God fails, their God is not trustworthy and abandons
    them.
Red-faced they come before non-believers,
Because I wasn't me, I wasn't him, them or her.
None of them are who they really are.
Forgotten, our proposition that faith makes life better
And, indeed, faith does make life infinitely better.
Every time we need from the gutters of our own minds,
Then God becomes helpless to us, in time:
He is no longer our hopeful divine.
By our consciences, let there be no fear or doubt but inner peace
And then, one day, we may rid the world of disease.

That which is disharmony to ours and God's universal plan.
He told us to enjoy the light inside;
We are all hanging on to a glimmer of hope outside.
In our goodness and not goodness so, we are specks of realness;
Illusion because we allow our self-awareness slip into
    nothingness.
Out of complete faith, without accepting anything

Because of our complete faith, we will get everything.
Peace, understanding, love, kindness
And be one in each other by self-awareness.
Instead of rejection, chaos, war or an inevitable mess,

Satan and his evil shadow is not God's but ours.
Mistrusting the divine by dwelling on guilt and shame in the
     tower –
The tower so difficult to leave.
The illusionary sins of Adam and Eve.
I am reaching out to God and humanity with kindness,
To overcome the lies and the inaccuracies of blindness,

That which has plunged us all into this mad destruction,
Faithless vision and the hypocrisy of religion's introductions.
Starved and famished before those many deceitful shrines,
Things evil existed only in poisoned minds.
Poisoned by the very force that was supposed to keep the world
     pure,
And all the trials and sufferings that goodness had to endure.
Laws that marked themselves by their own crooked state,
Turned each other against each other in states of hate.
We must strengthen the bridges of sorrow
For all our children of tomorrow.

Joni

Do they give us wings the moment we die?
Permission and resurrection to fly?
A very last chance to say goodbye?
Oh, when we die. Oh, when we die.
See Joni play in the new-born day.
The wind plays with her hair.
She's young; she doesn't have a care.
The sun warms her skin.
She feels so much from within.
Could she ever be a dying flame?
A dying flame in a dying game?
Far beyond these imaginary walls
Hangs a flower, a waterfall.
In the middle of the night, you can hear Joni call,
There is a monster coming up the hall.
A rainbow fall, a waterfall, I can play with Annabelle.
So many playgrounds, Joni has fell.
They seem to shut all the interest of the heart
And the leaking valves that no longer spark.
Don't leave poor Joni in the dark.
Don't leave the dreams in her mind.
She is too scared, far too kind,
In a world gone badly and madly blind.

Bring her to the garden, bring her flowers.
She lives under the umbrella of passing hours.
Under the umbrella of the insane,
Let no one detract her good name.
Joni is never at fault and she's never to blame.
She is cared for by the umbrella of the insane.
Concrete walls and polished wooden floors.
Don't let Joni bang the door.

Don't let Joni bang the door in rage.
This used not be Joni's playground stage.
Remembering the hurricane and the Holocaust –
Joni was barely born when millions were lost.
Keep her company while she plays:
There are monsters that try to keep warm her days.
Always be with Joni while she plays.

Stranger with the ice-cold body of frost,
Remember the hurricane and the Holocaust.
With shivering answers, in prayer, they offer their explanation:
Logic, rational and in rotation.
Be it the will of God,
Or maybe a world without a god.
Joni's wounds are starting to fester again.
Go with Joni to play with her train.
My hairs stand up and freeze behind my head:
They found Joni's little pony dead.
It had been whipped and kicked to death.
It once carried little Joni all across the Earth.
Give Joni her starting gun
But don' let Joni play with none.
Keep the monsters in the deep

While you hush little Joni off to sleep.
Soothe her heart if she starts to weep.
Joni's dolls face is cracked for centuries of being here
Yet, she's far too young for that filthy gossip we hear.
If the weeds live again, then the rivers will die again
But little Joni, she has always been –
Joni's that little bit too tender to have ever seen.
Anabelle, take Joni home again.
Keep her out of sight of all men.
Take her out today;
Let you and Joni go out to play.

Joni, part ii

Now that the skies have burst themselves open,
The dream down below is broken
But Joni's heart is open.
There are times, my nervous feet can't stand;
I can't find moments to read the cracks in my hands
But Joni is generous and kind –
Forgives unforgiveness blind.
Her senses bringing us back home to our healing.

Joni is healing; Joni is feeling.
Like a vision, she dances across the porch.
She falls softly into our touch.
Joni is not a tormented word on a blank page.
Neither is she a furnace in uncontrollable rage.
From the outsides of the cartoon labourers within,
Joni is too holy to sin.
At night, they play drunk rock on the streets
For flesh ghosts, too frightened to ever want to meet.
Joni too can be flesh, even though Joni doesn't eat.
It takes a man or a woman to apologise:
All of us who are wise and for all we despise.
Joni is not disguise.

Strangers dancing in and out of costumes.
Joni fills the air with sweet perfume.
Joni will tell you, you're never alone.
There's no such thing as an organ of stone.
For all the crippled feelings we bury inside,
I can feel Joni, she doesn't hide.
From our Mother Earth and our motherly heavenly sky,
Joni will release the tears we cry.
Joni isn't abrupt and neither is she shy.

For all that we are and all that we're not,
Joni's heart will never rot.

All of you who are left out in the cold,
Afraid of sickness, afraid of getting old,
Joni will take you warmly into her fold.
And when the seeds of the world have all gone,
We must believe in some place we can find our true song –
Some place safe with Joni, even though it's all gone badly wrong.
When you feel alone in a crowd or the traffic too loud,
Joni will be your shawl, your shroud.
If you end up in a hostel scrounging for a meal,
Joni will be there with her prayer wheel.

The body knows many ways to face the cold
But what does body know of the soul?
If our river banks ever do explode,
We'll have to kill one another for road.
Sleep, everyone with your blankets on.
Tomorrow is eternally gone.
All the powerless power and bitterness we dwell upon
For what we've lost and the real love that seems forever gone.
Annabelle will take Joni out today.
Annabelle and Joni will together play.
Right through the day and till the beginning of the night,
And their wings will reveal to the world, how to fly a kite.

What Am I?

The shape of the core determines the contour of the cover,
If you think of the onion and the orange.
But think, to get to the core is to destroy the cover.
Then the grace of that onion and the beauty of that orange,
Both tightly closed, are gone.
Do you still wish to peel to the layers of my soul?

About the Author

William Tiernan is a Galway-based poet and author. His writings reflect his personal experiences and convictions, as well as strong ties to the community in which he lives, his identification with the place where he grew up.

His first collection of poems, *Greetings from Guilka, Ballymoe: Poems from the Head and the Heart*, was published in 2016.

Previously, he was National Winner in the poetry category at the Hanna Greally International Literary Awards in 2014, organised as part of the annual SiarScéal Festival.